Change Leadership

To Christine, a constant source of help and support

Contents

List of Figures

Acknowledgements

There have been many people, in addition to my wife, Christine, who have assisted me in bringing this book to life. Naming just a few, Michael Loveless for the cartoons and photograph, Andrew Moffat, members of the Gower editing and production team, particularly Jonathan Norman, my business colleagues including Chris Lever, Ross Harling, Adrian Banger, Laura McHarrie, and Dennis Borden, for their continuing encouragement, especially during some trying times. Finally, family and friends who by "touching base" have helped to keep me on track.

Preface

WHAT IS A CHANGE-ADEPT ORGANIZATION?

During the past decade my research into organizational creativity, innovation and change leadership, has indicated that:

- Everybody from the boardroom to the shop floor feel the rate of change is increasing, year on year.

- Neither an organization's size nor its industry sector appears to have an influence on its capability to change.

- A person's position/role in the organization appears to influence their perception of their organization's change capability.

- There exist significant differences between organizations that are successful at responding to change when compared to those that were not successful. I have classed these two distinct types of organization as being either Change-Adept (able to continuously change faster than their competitors) or Change-Inept (unable to respond to the challenges faced).

- Twenty significant distinguishing characteristics for each organizational type, summarized in Table 1, were identified; the research also showed that:

  - People from Change-Adept organizations feel fully involved in the changes and highly positive about the organization.

People from Change-Inept organizations feel excluded and were very negative about their organization. A major difference between the Change-Adept and Change-Inept was their project success rates, with the Change-Adept organizations running at over 80 per cent compared to less than 20 per cent success for the Change-Inept; success being defined as achieving the goals agreed upon at the project's commencement.

Table 1: Adept/Inept Comparisons

Profile Element	Change-Adept	Change-Inept
Feeling	8.36	2.78
Experience/Education	7.64	3.00
Environment	8.18	3.56
Leadership	7.91	2.61
Incentives	7.91	4.56
Plans	7.82	2.44
Sense of Involvement	7.64	2.33
TOTAL (max 63)	**55.46**	**21.28**

- A Change-Adept organization might be described as a Nimble Jaguar, fleet of foot, focussed and able to rapidly change direction in pursuit of its goal[1] whereas the Change-Inept organization may be considered to be a Braying Mule, lots of noise with very little movement. In the former, employees' resistance to change is low and the motivators for change are high, whilst in the latter personal resistance is high and motivation for change low. You may wish to consider what type of animal might best describe an organization where the employees are *excited by* and *up for change* but there is no motivation provided for change.

- As an example, in the mid 1990s a very successful wine merchant's chain decided to significantly up-skill their store staff: "One of the probable reasons was because training and personal development had received a great deal of attention in both professional journals and the business press." They spent a considerable amount of money with a training company to put all their managers through a two-day course. Unfortunately they had omitted to align this to their business strategy and so were unable to provide the necessary focus to motivate the managers to move in the right direction. In fact the managers appeared to have little or no idea of how they should apply their newly acquired skills. The outcome being that the managers either found themselves new jobs or partners. The whole exercise cost the company a million pounds and achieved very little.

OTHER FINDINGS

The research also confirmed that a leader's style and approach is one of the most crucial elements in organizational change. With this in mind, this workbook aims to help the reader better understand the nature of change, and then provides some approaches and tools/techniques that help the leader to raise their game and in doing so develop a Change-Adept organization.

Martin Orridge
January 2008

---

1   See Appendix.

Introduction

CHANGE IS THE ONLY CONSTANT

As I look back at my working life I've come to believe that Benjamin Franklin's famous quote should be amended to, "In this world, nothing is certain but *change*, death and taxes." And, if we are to believe what some of today's scientists are suggesting, then death is now considerably less certain than in Benjamin Franklin's time and, if you are to accept as true some commentators' observations, that today's corporations are very adept at avoiding taxes, then the most certain of the three is change.

In today's business world it is not the Grim Reaper, but Change who sits constantly at our shoulder. It could be said that the Grim Reaper generally only appears if we have failed to heed the voice of Change. If I consider the six organizations where I worked, only two now remain, the others lost their identities after takeovers and/or restructuring. The two that remain have acquired, sold, re-engineered, down-sized, right-sized, process improved, merged and de-merged many times, so that even though the name remains, what lies beneath the corporate wrapper is considerably different to when I was there. The press are constantly reporting change and attempts to change. As I write this, I note that there are many column inches of the weekend business newspapers devoted to the UK public services modernization debate. And, over the years, these same newspapers have covered the decline of the UK's heavy industry, manufacturing, car industry and national airlines, the rise of the service sector, the rise and fall of biotechnology and e-commerce, the emergence of China (to replace Japan) and the need to improve the road and rail infrastructure. There will have been similar articles and debate throughout most of the industrialized world and if you use these same newspapers to look at today's company stock market listings compared to those of 15 years ago, many names are no longer there.

Like all other species on earth, long-term corporate survival is an excellent, perhaps the only, measure of success. It is those organizations that have continually transformed themselves to meet the new business challenges that have endured, whilst the also-rans' legacy is confined to the history books.

However, it is all too easy to discuss organizational change in abstraction, particularly when you are dealing with large corporations with vast product ranges across global markets. Somewhere within these structures there are people, and it is often the human aspects of change that are the most difficult to manage. To this end, a constant theme throughout the book will be on these human aspects and how we, as change leaders, can create this complex, yet highly flexible and adaptable entity, cope with change and in turn help ensure their organization's long-term survival.

1 A Little Theory Concerning Personal and Organizational Change

This chapter of the book examines how change affects both the individual and the whole organization. We commence with an examination of how we are still conditioned by our forefathers' survival behaviours. And, having looked at the individual level we will move on to study how groups of individuals, who comprise an organization, have an effect on its ability to change.

Note: There are a number of exercises throughout the book. Please have a pen and paper available before you start to read and having recorded your answers keep them available for when you read the subsequent chapters.

PERSONAL CHANGE

Our Ancestors' Influence

Imagine, if you will, a grassy plain with a few bushes and trees dotted on it. Coming along a track on the plain is a man dressed in animal skins, carrying a spear and the carcase of a small, deer-like creature slung over his shoulders. The sun has just set making the sky a shade of pale coral behind him. He is silhouetted against the pink canvas as he moves as fast as he can towards an escarpment, which is about two kilometres away. Peering into the distance he can just make out the flickering light of a fire at a cave entrance, a fire on which to cook his kill, a very important kill because the family group has been without fresh meat for several days, he can almost taste the cooked flesh when suddenly there appears a sabre-toothed tiger ahead of him.

What do you think could happen next?

There are a number of possible outcomes, which fall into three categories:

The caveman becomes rooted to the spot – Shock – Frozen

Figure 1.1   The Frozen Caveman

The caveman runs away – Flight

Figure 1.2   The Caveman in Flight

The caveman attacks the sabre-toothed tiger – Fight

Figure 1.3   The Fighting Caveman

It is, of course, possible that all three may occur, whereby the caveman is initially immobile, then fights, because the need for food is urgent, and finally flees if he is liable to lose his life. But, whatever the outcome of this particular scene, it is these typical responses that have contributed to our survival on this planet.

What is our Body Doing?

Our brain

Before reading on, spend a few moments thinking about the times you were really surprised or shocked by something totally unexpected. How did you feel immediately and how did you feel and/or react a short while later?

When something completely unexpected occurs we are shocked and when we are in shock we are temporarily immobilized as our brain attempts to understand what has occurred. Often we will react instinctively, for example, by leaping out of the way of an oncoming motor vehicle or, if our self-preservation behaviours have not engaged, we may become rooted to the spot and be run over.

When a sudden surprise or shock happens to us it may take up to ten seconds or so, before we can behave rationally – rather than just instinctively.

It is for this very reason that disaster scenarios, like an oil rig supply helicopter coming down in the sea, are rehearsed with both crew and rig workers. In this life-threatening circumstance you do not want passengers and crew to be either immobilized or reacting instinctively to preserve their own life.

How many times have you looked back at an unexpected event and regretted saying the first thing that came into your head or how you immediately reacted to a situation. A good rule in non life-threatening situations is to count to ten before saying or doing anything. Watching how politicians handle the unexpected question is a good example of how we might wish to behave when surprised. Next time you listen to the news, or watch a current affairs programme and there is a politician being pressed by an eager commentator, watch how they start their reply without answering the question. It may be along the line of: "That is a very good question, only the other day when I was in my constituency I was asked something quite similar … and so on." These well rehearsed lines are delivered using their autopilot and as they trot out these prepared lines, they can start thinking about how they might answer the posed question, if they choose to answer it at all!

So to summarize, as the old saying goes, "Always engage brain before putting mouth into gear."

The rest of our body

Once the initial shock has passed we move to the fight or flight phase. Although these are outwardly entirely different outcomes, our body is behaving in very similar ways. Adrenalin starts to flow, heart rate and respiration increases and blood is pumped at an increased rate to the major muscle groups, whilst being reduced for organs that are not immediately required for fighting or fleeing. In the flight (fearing for life) situation the body may also attempt to reduce weight by defecation and urination. These automatic responses helped our forefathers survive sabre-toothed tigers and any other daily life-threatening crisis they may have faced.

Our 21st-century sabre-toothed tigers may be the report that has to be completed by yesterday, the departmental re-organization, or an irate customer, and in these situations our bodies behave in just the same way as the caveman carrying the deer. However, in today's business world we do not run away or punch our customer/boss/supplier on the nose (well not usually). Instead we suffer from stress, insomnia and ulcers as we suppress our natural tendencies for dealing with these modern-day threats.

Stress and illness

Since the 1950s a great deal of research has been undertaken exploring the relationship between stress and illness. One example of research being *The Social Readjustment Rating Scale*[1] developed by Holmes and Rahe. In this work individuals were asked to mark all the events, from a list of 43, which have occurred in their lives over the previous 12 months. Each event was weighed according to life change units ranging from 11, a minor violation of the law, for example, a speeding ticket, to 100, the death of a partner; with other events such as being promoted, getting married and taking out a mortgage lying between the two extremes.

Holmes and Rahe suggested that individuals reporting life change units totalling less than 150 points should be in generally good health the following year. If the total exceeded 150, but is less than 300, the individual has about a 50 per cent chance of developing a serious illness the following year. Among individuals with scores above 300 units, the chance of developing a serious illness rises to 70 per cent.

It can be no wonder, as the rate of change in our lives increases, that over the past 15 years stress management has become such a lucrative business. Open any health magazine, or even many business journals and you will find stress counsellors and gurus offering a whole range of relaxation and/or physical exercise activities to help provide a release for the body's natural threat coping tendencies.

---

1   T. H. Holmes and R. H. Rahe (1967), "The Social Readjustment Rating Scale", *Journal of Psychosomatic Research*.

The Kübler-Ross Transition Curve

Whenever a life event happens we are undergoing some sort of a change. It does not matter whether it is a pleasant one, like being promoted, or an unpleasant one, like divorce, our feelings and our ability to cope will go through the same cycle or transition phases. These transition phases can be thought of as a curve (Figure 1.4) which passes through seven stages. It is known as the Kübler-Ross Transition Curve which is based on studies of personal bereavement. This work was then used as a basis to explore people's feelings during business and organizational change.

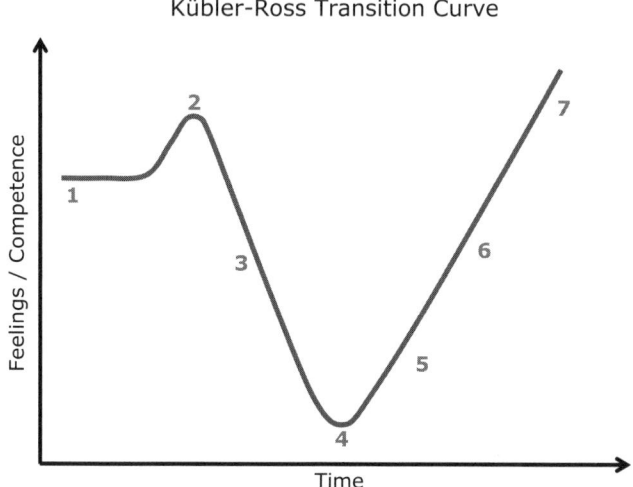

Kübler-Ross Transition Curve

Figure 1.4   The Personal Dip Curve

Stage 1 – Shock or immobilization

This aspect, which was also discussed earlier in *fight* or *flight*, is where we have the feeling of being overwhelmed, or being unable to make plans, unable to reason and unable to understand. Many people experience this as a feeling of being frozen by indecision.

Note: There is often a phase prior to Stage 1. I call this the Anticipation or Rumour Phase, where we expect something to happen or be announced. During this phase we may oscillate between feeling elated or despondent when we hear the latest rumour or are waiting for something to happen. It is like going through a complete transition cycle both quickly and frequently. This can be very debilitating for an organization if a lot of its people's energy is used up in response to rumours.

Mini exercise

As leaders, though not just as leaders, there will be times when we are surprised perhaps during difficult and complex negotiations with business associates, trade union leaders or even the press or media. When this occurs there are two possible outcomes:

- we say the first thing that springs to mind, or

- stand there, looking like a goldfish, whilst we come up with an answer.

As you can see both may have undesirable outcomes. We need to give ourselves time to think but not at the expense of looking foolish. One executive I knew always took a plastic cup containing a small amount of water which he would knock over if his adversary used shock tactics in an attempt to gain an advantage. Whilst the spill was being mopped up he had created some time to think of his response.

What you are required to do in this exercise is to prepare a form of words to create the *mop up* time that enables you prepare the response you would wish to give and thereby appear in total control of the situation. Politicians are masters at doing this. When posed the difficult question they may well respond, "Well Brian, that is an interesting question, only the other day I was asked something similar by a constituent when I was running my weekly surgery, I believe that … and so on, and so on." The response has been learnt verbatim and provides time for you to think about what you wish to say. Obviously we cannot keep using the same set of words as it will soon be obvious to all what we are doing. Repeating the question may also be an approach or you may adopt the Harold Wilson[2] strategy of either drawing thoughtfully on your pipe or tamping some tobacco down into the pipe bowl. He was a man in control of the situation but rather more difficult in these days of tougher smoking restrictions. But I guess you have got the point. Your exercise, therefore, is to prepare a set of words that can buy you a vital ten seconds and then learn them by heart. It is a lot less messy than knocking over the proverbial cup of water and may be used anywhere in just about any situation.

Stage 2 – Denial or minimization

This is the way of getting out of the first stage. Minimize the change. See it as trivial. Very often we will deny that a change even exists. We may continue following our old routines or tell ourselves: "I'm not affected by this" or "The information I received must be wrong." Denial provides time for temporary retreat from reality while we build up our internal strength.

Stage 3 – Incompetence or depression

As we become aware that we must make some change in the way we are doing our job or living, and become more aware of the new realities, we begin to recognize that we may find it difficult to cope in the new situation or job. We will then begin to become depressed. We are facing up to the fact that there has been a change. This is the time when it is difficult to know how to cope

---

2   UK Prime Minister, 1963–76.

with the problems, changes and life in general. In line with our inner feelings our competence to cope in this new situation also diminishes.

Stage 4 – Acceptance or letting go

As we become more aware of reality, we start accepting it for what it is. Through the first three stages there is still an attachment to the past, a looking backwards and inwards. Moving to stage four there is a letting go of the past. We may say or think: "OK, here I am now, here is what I have; here is what I want." As we accept this, our feelings begin to rise and we start to become more optimistic about the situation. During the next three stages we are thinking about the future, a looking forwards and outwards.

Stage 5 – Testing

Having accepted the situation and let go, we become more active and start testing ourselves in relation to the new situation: trying out new behaviours, new lifestyles, and so on. We can have a lot of new-found energy as we are testing out new things.

Stage 6 – Search for meaning or understanding

After our outbursts of activity and self-testing we start to gradually shift towards becoming concerned with understanding how and why things are different. At this stage we try to understand our earlier behaviour, for example, our anger and/or our depression. During this stage our competence may rapidly increase.

Stage 7 – Internalization

When we are able to step back and stop trying to understand everything, is when we can move to the final stage of a transition. Now we can incorporate what we have learned into our daily life. The change becomes part of us. There is an understanding and acceptance.

These seven transition stages represent a cycle of experiencing a disruption, gradually acknowledging its reality, testing ourselves, and incorporating changes into our behaviour. For a major life change event it seems to take around 18 months to two years to move through the complete cycle and it is possible to get stuck in any of the early stages.

Implications of the transition curve for change programmes

The transition curve identifies a number of things that change leaders should consider when planning for change:

- We are all individuals and will move through the cycle at different rates.

- Introducing a new programme before we have reached the acceptance stage of a previous programme may have a compounding effect on incompetence and depression.

- We have lives outside of our organization and the change programme may not be the only major life event that is happening to us. This may influence our progression through the cycle.

- Senior management, particularly those who have been involved with the planning of a major change programme, will be many months ahead on the cycle compared to the rest of the organization. They will often forget this fact and become frustrated at the slow progress of the rest of us.

- We cannot avoid the cycle, we can only take actions that may reduce its depth and/or help us move through each stage more quickly.

Exercises 1 and 2

Consider a change that has recently happened to you, draw the transition curve and put an "X" where you think you are on the curve. Make a list of your feelings and behaviours that are a result of your position on the curve.

Imagine you are a change leader and that you are introducing a new computer system into your department. For each of the first six transition curve stages, list the types of activities or actions you might undertake to help members of your team move forward to the next stage.

ORGANIZATIONAL CHANGE

Extending the Transition Curve

The sum of the individuals

In the previous section we discussed how we, as individuals, go through the transition cycle. If we consider that an organization is comprised of a large number of individuals, each of whom is moving through their own curve, then the cycle for the organization will describe a similar path with individuals each at different points on the overall curve (Figure 1.5).

Figure 1.5 illustrates the lag that will occur between the board and staff as knowledge of a change programme is cascaded down the organization. The reader may wish to consider the implications of this lag.

Share price big dipper

The change curve can be extended a stage further if we consider it for an organization's board of directors or senior leadership team. If we plot their competence on the vertical axis we can see that, should a major change occur in their industry, the group will also follow the same cycle. The precise shape of the curve they follow will depend on how rapidly they learn about and respond to the new situation with which they are faced.

Often a successful company may initially deny that the external event has caused the crisis and may issue statements such as their strength in the

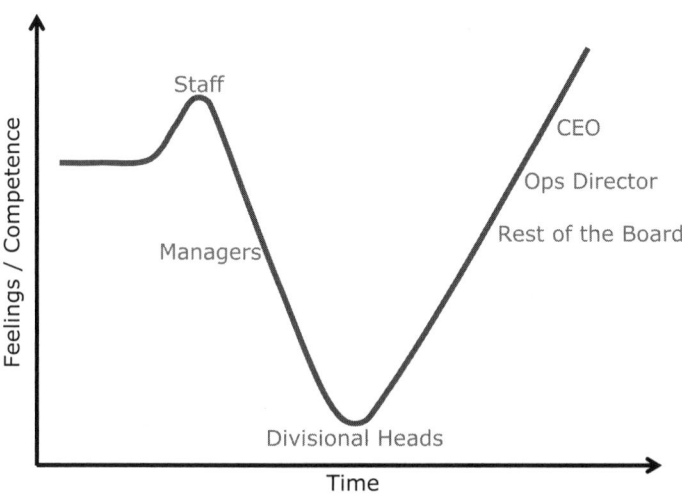

Figure 1.5   The Organizational Dip Curve

market will see them through, or new products (that have been based on the old paradigms) will address this problem. After the denial stage the senior management team start to slide down the slope of incompetence. If they learn quickly they will take appropriate actions and the curve follows the traditional single dip path. However, there are occasions when senior management are initially complacent, or they take action based on the old inappropriate mental models. The slide will continue (Figure 1.6), often with mini upturns, as each inappropriate rescue plan is tried, until corporate failure occurs, or there is real learning and appropriate actions are taken and recovery ensues. As investor confidence is a measure of management competence, the share price will follow the same downward dipping path.

Needless to say this may not be just confined to the boardroom, and individuals or groups at any level in an organization may exhibit similar behaviours that may have a significant influence on the pace of change.

Exercise 3

Make a list of some of the signs that may give you clues as to whether or not an individual or group are fully engaged in a change programme.

The Innovation Curve

When a new idea or change is introduced, whether it is bringing a new product to the market, or introducing new ways of working, its acceptance by the target population, or organization, will follow an "S"-shaped curve (Figure 1.7).

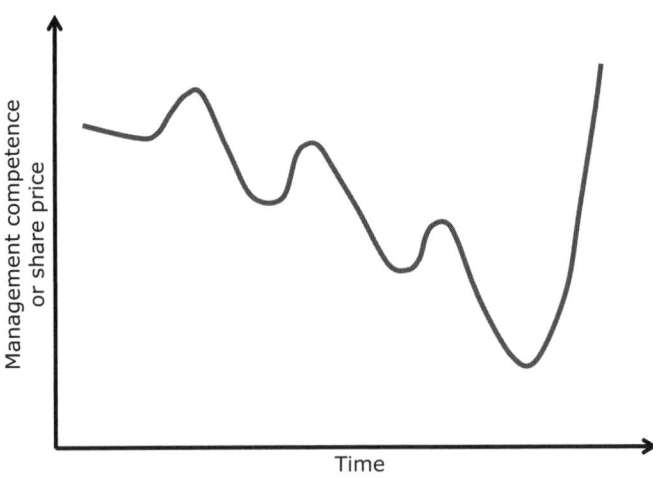

Figure 1.6 **The Share Price Dip Curve**

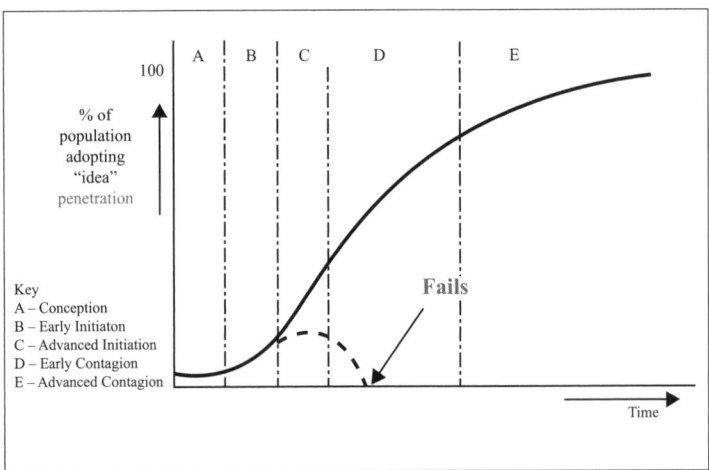

Figure 1.7 **An Organization's Acceptance of Innovation and Change**

The "S" curve phases are:

Conception
Conception describes the phase when the innovation, or change, is embryonic and introduced to the organization for the first time. During this phase only an extremely small percentage of the organization will accept the change.

Early initiation
During the early initiation phase the growth in acceptance of the innovation, or change, finally starts with the early adopters in the population trying it out. Early adopters will typically try anything and everything. Consequently, managing the end of this phase is critical for the overall acceptance of the change, as it is necessary for the early adopter trailblazer to be followed by many more people. If, at this point, the population at large does not start to

accept the change then it will follow the most common path (dotted line) to failure. It is possible for an innovation or change programme to stall during the subsequent phases, but it is more usually because a new and *better* idea/initiative has become available. Exciting and original change initiatives have been known to fail because management has not allowed sufficient time, or provided sufficient resources, for it to take hold and, having lost their nerve, initiate another new programme. This can result in a continuing downward spiral, as increasingly frenetic programmes are introduced in rapid succession.

Advanced initiation

During advanced initiation the curve becomes steeper with more and more of the organization accepting the change. Again, it is still possible for the change to fail during this phase, as a critical mass of the population has not yet been won over.

Early contagion

The bulk of the population adopts the idea during the early contagion phase. These people are seen as the followers of the idea compared to the leaders of the initiation phases.

Advanced contagion

In general terms, the advanced contagion phase covers the last 15–20 per cent of the population who are the late adopters of the change. A significant amount of effort may be required to ensure this section of population adopts it.

Exercise 4

Using the innovation "S" curve model, list what activities a change leader might undertake during each phase of the curve to ensure their change project progresses from conception to advanced contagion.

Change Readiness – Individuals

The final model we will examine (Figure 1.8) is the change readiness of both individuals and groups.

| Resistant | Reluctant | Receptive |

Figure 1.8   **Change Readiness of Groups and Individuals**

This model suggests that there are three possible behavioural states for an individual to experience when considering a proposed change. They may be resistant, reluctant, or receptive to the change. Where they are in the spectrum will determine their actions.

Exercise 5

For each of the categories – resistant, reluctant and receptive – make a list of how you believe a person from that category would behave, overtly and covertly, to a proposed major change.

A person's underlying personality will have an influence on how they act to a proposal. Consider someone who is energetic, outgoing and likes to be at the centre of things and compare them to someone who is quieter, more inward looking and thoughtful. They will outwardly react to things in a different way.

Exercise 6

Review your lists from Exercise 5, think about these two personality types and put an "O" beside the items on your list that you think are appropriate to outgoing people and an "I" next to those items you think are appropriate to inward-looking people. If you have any additional ideas about people's different behaviour towards change, add them to your list.

Change Readiness – Groups

Most people in your organization will belong to a group or number of different groups, some formal and many informal. These small groups may also range across the highly resistant to highly receptive spectrum.

Within these groups there will be leaders and followers. Leaders, as the name implies, can have a major influence on whether or not their group will respond positively to a proposed change. Also, group leadership may or may not necessarily be aligned to a job title or grade; a person's power to influence may spring from their personality, that is their innate leadership qualities, or it may be they have expert knowledge, or they are in a position to reward or punish other group members.

Group leaders, like the early adopter trailblazers mentioned in the previous section, are key to building up early momentum in a change project.

Exercise 7

Make a list of activities that you might undertake as a change leader to make people less resistant to a proposed change. Review your list and mark against each activity an "I" if it is appropriate for individuals, an "L" if it is appropriate for leaders, a "G" if it is appropriate for groups, or an "A" if it is appropriate to all categories.

What Next!?

During this first chapter of the book you should have completed seven exercises. When reading Chapter 2 use your responses to the questions as a cross-check. Are there any ideas and activities that you have recorded that are not mentioned in Chapter 2, Moving the Organization?

2 Moving the Organization

In Chapter 1 we explored how change affects people in different ways:

- Change is personal.

- Sudden change may shock and immobilize.

- People may try to avoid change, run away from it or fight it.

- Change can be very stressful.

- Everybody will go through the change cycle, some faster than others.

- A few people, the trailblazers, will be highly receptive to innovation and change.

- A few people will be highly resistant to a proposed change.

- Most people lie between the two extremes and will be generally reluctant to change.

- Formal and informal group leaders can influence people's willingness or otherwise to change.

In this chapter we will examine a model to support organizational transformation.

A MODEL FOR SUCCEEDING AT CHANGE

The model is founded on the works of Drucker, Hertzberg, Lawrence, Maslow and Weisbord, all of whom have researched and written extensively about both individual and organizational change. Although some of their work is 50 years old, it is still as relevant today as it was when first published. In fact, it can be said that these are ideas that have stood the sternest test, the test of time.

Resistors and Motivators

In Chapter 1 we noted that change is personal and that we each make our own individual journey to the new world or order of things. How resistant we are to a proposed change will depend on the type of person we are, whom we work with and are influenced by, what is going on in the rest of our life and how the personal impact of the proposed change is perceived. The greater the resistance we feel against a change, the less likely we are to accept and/or adopt the change. These are the Resistors. Motivators, on the other hand, are those activities that we undertake to help somebody accept and/or adopt a change. However, if their resistance is too high applying motivators will be ineffective and can even be counterproductive.

To illustrate this point, consider the metaphor of a family saloon car and a smooth or rocky road. In this instance the Resistor is the surface, that is the type of road or track the car is on, and the Motivator is the accelerator or gas pedal. First of all consider the case when the stationary car stands on smooth road (and for all you physicists – but not perfectly smooth). If you apply the accelerator, or gas, the car will move off, having first put it into gear and released the handbrake! The more you depress the accelerator the faster you will go and the less time it takes to reach your destination.

Now consider the car on a rocky track. When there are just a few rocks then, if you drive more slowly and steer carefully, you can make progress. However, if there are lots of large rocks they will have to be removed from the road before you can make any real progress, and until they are removed using the accelerator is ineffective. It is also worth considering the case when there are many small rocks and you use too much accelerator – you make some initial progress, but if you try to go too fast the car is likely to disintegrate!

So, if you wish to succeed with your change programme you must initially work at reducing resistance to a point where the motivators can work to bring about the desired change.

Another way to look at this is that you need to invest, pay a fee, in the initial groundwork before offering motivational words of encouragement to change, using your lips.

FEE and LIPS – Managing Continual Transformation

There are seven elements that need to be managed if successful transformation is to be achieved. The first three, Feelings, Experience and Environment, address the resistance aspects; with the remaining four, Leadership, Incentives, Plans and a Sense of Involvement refer to the motivators that should be applied.

FEE

As already mentioned FEE stands for Feelings, Experience and Environment and is the necessary stake or *ante* to enter the change game. Over the years you will probably have seen films, when a card player did not bring a sufficient stake for the poker game and has to *fold* when they had the winning hand. The same is true for change programmes, and the initial stake necessary to lay the foundations for successful sustainable transformation can be quite high.

Feelings

If people are to be motivated to change then they need to harbour positive attitudes and beliefs towards themselves, the organization and its leadership.

Fear of the unknown, confidence in the leadership and past experiences will have a major influence on how individuals feel. Clarity of vision and purpose (see also Leadership) can help people to be more positive, and less resistant, about the future. An experience of a successful change, or real learning from a not so successful one, is likely to make them more positive towards any further changes.

Experience

Winston Churchill's statement of "Give us the tools and we will finish the job" (Radio broadcast, 9 February 1941) is just as applicable now as it was then. If we want people to behave and/or work differently then they must have the *tools* or the means of making the tools available, before the change is embarked upon.

To maintain low resistance to change we need to ensure that staff have the appropriate skills, knowledge and competencies in place, or the means of rapid acquisition, which will enable them to perform effectively in the *new world*.

Environment

Environment works at two levels. First, there is the underlying culture of the organization and second, there are the actual work structures and business procedures/processes that are in place to support change. Creating an environment where people feel they will be helped and supported during the change underpins the other two elements.

LIPS

Low personal resistance to change is but the first step, to make real transformation happen we need also to apply the LIPS motivators.

Leadership

Leadership works at a number of points within the organization. It is critical for senior managers to demonstrate leadership in both their words and actions. Confidence in our leaders is critical when we are about to embark into the unknown. Leadership at the team/group level that is consistent with the senior team is also a key element, as they will often be seen as the senior team's proxy.

Leaders need to ensure that their vision has been communicated and understood and that people's own personal visions map on to the corporate one. Once there is a commonality of vision there is an increased likelihood that there will be clearly defined goals at all levels of the organization.

Incentives

Incentives do not necessarily mean financial rewards. A timely and appropriate word can work wonders as can the example set by the organization's leaders.

Unfortunately, financial reward can become the common negotiation currency that, as the lowest common organizational denominator, all too often fails to inspire and motivate. This is because it may not address the real issues.

Incentives will often be a mixture of carrot and stick, like the Israelites' exodus from Egypt: they had the carrot of the Promised Land and the stick of hard labour and the plagues in Egypt. The most successful leaders remind their people that the pain they are currently experiencing is likely to get worse as well as providing a vision of the new world they will be moving towards.

All the eyes of the organization will be on the trailblazers; those involved in the early pilots or are first to adopt the new way, and, if they are seen to have been offered appropriate incentives and rewards, then the rest of the organization is more likely to follow.

Plans

Planning operates on two levels, the outline overall plan of how to achieve the intended goal, and the very detailed short-term ones covering the first steps or next steps of the programme. Detailed short-term plans, covering between three to six months, will both inspire confidence and ensure good management control.

Sense of involvement

When we have a sense of involvement in the change we will feel we have more control over our future. When we feel we have some control over our own destiny then we are much more likely to be committed to it. This sense of involvement can be achieved by providing those affected with the opportunity to contribute to the change.

Wherever possible let staff work out the detail. They will probably be better at it than senior management as they live with the detail on a daily basis. For example, if you are moving offices let the staff be involved with the seating plans and décor in line with an overall plan and/or budget; once engaged, change will be far easier.

Exercise 8

Successful transformation requires every one of the elements contained in FEE and LIPS to be present. Think about each element and list how you believe people might behave if it was not present? Some suggestions are shown in Figure 2.1.

Consequences of Missing Elements

Successful change requires every element to be present.
There are consequences associated with each one that is missing.

F	-	**Resistance and guerrilla actions.**
E	-	**Anxiety, frustration, unable to cope.**
E	-	**False assumptions, duplicated effort, turf issues.**
L	-	**No momentum, fizzles out.**
I	-	**Why bother?**
P	-	**Haphazard, no focus, duplicated effort, gaps.**
S	-	**Slow, "why us?", passive resistance.**

Figure 2.1   Consequences of Missing Elements

THE ART OF CHANGE LEADERSHIP

In the last section, FEE and LIPS provided an overarching framework for successful organizational transformation. In Chapter 3, 75 actions, based on FEE and LIPS, are provided to help lower people's resistance and provide motivation for change. It could be said that all the other chapters provide a useful recipe for successful business transformation. But, just possessing a recipe is no guarantee of a successful dish – to produce a culinary masterpiece one also needs an accomplished chef. To better understand the role of the *organizational chef* this section will examine some of the tools, techniques and skills that need to be applied to the organizational transformation recipe – it will explore the art of change leadership.

What is Leadership?

If there is a leader, then there are followers. If people are to follow someone then their leadership must be considered as something personal, a relationship between the leader and follower, with the leader's credibility providing the foundation. There needs to be trust established between leader and follower.

At the beginning of this relationship a leader is *known* by their words, but very quickly they will be *judged* by their deeds. Successful leaders inspire action and deliver worthwhile results. They are able to balance their rhetoric with action. Leaders also recognize that to succeed they will have to invest significant amounts of their personal credibility in the knowledge that only success pays dividends and therefore increases their credibility. This, in turn, enables them to reinvest still more and drive the change forward.

Exercise 9

Select three leaders from the present or past; from any walk of life, for example, business, political, military or religious and so on. Using a separate A4 (quarto) sheet of paper for each leader, write the name of each leader at the top of the sheet. For each leader in turn write down, if you know:

- What event or events led them to become a leader, and then list;

- Why you believed they are/were a credible leader, then write;

- How they used words to inspire *followership*, and;

- What actions resulted that were seen as beneficial to their *organization;*

- If they are no longer a leader you may also wish to write down how this came to pass.

Now review the three leaders and look for any common features between them, particularly the skills and other attributes they employed whilst leading. Finally take a fresh sheet of paper and make a list of the skills, knowledge and experience that would make your perfect leader. Consider which of your skills you would like to develop to increase your leadership potential.

Loading the change for success: imagine the change programme is like a military campaign. Just like the best generals, you should plan and develop a strategy that is loaded in your favour. Take time to understand the opposition so you can play to your strength and their weakness.

Planning the Rate of Change

Successful organizations continually transform themselves as they respond to, or anticipate, the changing environment. Sometimes the rate of change will require speed and sometimes it may need to be slower. When planning for change the leader needs to consider:

- How much short-term risk is there to the organization?

- How much resistance is expected?

- Who has the power?

- How much commitment is needed?

If the organization's survival is at risk then change needs to be fast. But, if there is likely to be a great deal of resistance then the pace may need to be slow. Using the template in Figure 2.2 may help you decide the rate at which you should try to proceed.

Speed	Fast	5	4	3	2	Slow	
1. What is the degree of short-term risk to the organization?							
Survival at risk							Low level of short-term risk
2. How much resistance is expected?							
Hardly any resistance							A great deal of resistance
3. Where is the power?							
You have all the power							You have virtually no power
4. How much commitment is required?							
Hardly any (Tell them)							A great deal (Involve them)

Figure 2.2   An Organization's Speed of Change

Mini exercise

- Answer each question and mark on the grid at what rate the pace of change should progress. Review the chart and decide:

- The requisite pace of change and the actions required to ensure each element progresses at the desired rate.

Driving through a change in response to a crisis will often require less effort compared to implementing an anticipatory change. But change based on moving from crisis to crisis will, in the long-term, exhaust the organization. Whereas, organizations that are able to continually transform will apply the extra effort required to drive anticipatory change. Always remember that the perception of the speed of change is different if you are a decision-maker compared to someone affected by the change.

Change – Intentional or Imposed

When responsible leaders see areas needing improvement, they carefully think through changes that they believe are for the good of the overall organization.

However, the changes they decide upon must be implemented by others from within the organization who have not been part of the original analysis and decision-making. For them, this becomes *imposed change*; it has a very different impact on people who choose to change.

For those who make the decisions, it is intentional change and it is seen as:

- Gradual;

- Incremental;

- Paced;

- Problem solving;

- The result of conscious decisions;

- Anticipated;

- Providing new opportunities.

Whereas, for those who are required to implement the change, it is an imposition and it is seen as:

- Sudden;

- Dramatic;

- Rapid and out of control;

- Creating problems;

- Denying choice;

- Unexpected;

- Disruptive to current routines.

Finding Allies and Using Other Leaders

Successful transformation requires engagement and the harnessing of leaders at all levels of the organization. These leaders may be found anywhere and everywhere, but the organization chart may not be the best way of locating them. Instead consider some of the traits you listed in the earlier exercise. They may well have included visionary, energetic, prepared to take risks, challenge the status quo, driven, always learning and with an ability to seize the moment.

You will increase your likelihood of success if you can identify people who demonstrate these traits and then engage and involve them in the change. Such people are looked to by their peers and if they adopt the change the others will very likely follow. Similarly, if they are not engaged they can slow, or even halt, progress.

Exercise 10

Using the template provided in Table 2.1, list all the key player(s) affected by your change and indicate their current and desired level of commitment (X = present position; O = desired position). If you do not know their current level of commitment, what does it tell you about your planning to date and how are you going to find out more?

Table 2.1   Level of Commitment Matrix

Key Individuals/ Stakeholders	Level of Commitment				
	Opposed	Indifferent	Allow	Will Help	Will Lead

Having identified the required movement, it is necessary to develop strategies to progress each stakeholder to the desired position. The strategies should be based on the organizational influence the individual possesses and their personalities/behaviours. Often it will require a combination of pushing and pulling them towards your goal. Table 2.2 illustrates how the empty matrix may be completed.

Table 2.2   Level of Commitment Matrix

Key Individuals/ Stakeholders	Level of Commitment				
	Opposed	Indifferent	Allow	Will Help	Will Lead
Customer X		X	O		
Supplier Y	X		O		
Production			X		O
Sales		X		O	
Manager Z		X			O

Push and Pull Influencing Styles

Your behaviour also has consequences as to how you get things done. You need to understand each of these stakeholders and their respective points of view. To achieve this requires an extraordinary level of rapport, involving thought, feeling, energy and insight. You also need to adapt to the working style of these key individuals.

The two primary styles of engagement are the:

1. *Pull style* – a responsive, drawing out style; and

2. *Push style* – an assertive, thrusting style.

When people engage they use a mixture of *push* and *pull* styles. To engage effectively with the key individuals you need to appreciate both your own and their preferred working and influencing style.

Those with a predominantly:

*   high *push style* tend to be quick, decisive and assertive;

*   low *push style* tend to be careful and take their time;

*   high *pull style* tend to focus on people's feelings and emotions;

*   low *pull style* tend to focus on the task, facts and logic.

The matrix in Figure 2.3 provides some approaches that will enable you to engage with and influence the different types.

	AMIABLE	**EXPRESSIVE**
High PULL (Outgoing) • People • Feelings • Emotions	• Trust important • Take time • Listen • Get to know them • Let them get to know you • Self disclose	• Give them the vision • Let them experience the new way • Let them talk to others who have succeeded • Make it fun
	ANALYTICAL	**DRIVER**
Low PULL (Reserved) • Task • Logic • Facts	• Facts are important • Take time • Give them all the detail • Let them learn	• Give them a short summary of benefits • Highlight the quick returns where time and money are saved • Give them the opportunity to lead
	Low PUSH (Ask) Quiet, Careful, Take time	**High PUSH (Tell)** Assertive, Quick, Decisive

Figure 2.3   Influencing Strategies for Different Personality Types

Whilst we are a mixture of the four personality types we usually have a preferred or predominant style. For example a person may predominantly be a Driver. But in many cases our primary style will be supported by one of the others, for example, a person may be an *analytical/amiable* – facts and details are the most important but they will also want to get to know the person behind the facts. Knowing a stakeholder's preferred style(s) will enable you to influence and motivate them to support the change.

Driving Change Using Push

Using *push* to bring about change is about increasing the forces for change. There are degrees of *push* that may be used to bring about change.

The lowest level of *push* force involves simply providing information to show the logic for change.

A moderate degree of *push* means pointing out the benefits that will accrue by adopting the change. Additional and incremental benefits may also be highlighted in an attempt to encourage (bribe) people to change.

The strongest degree of *push* implies emphasizing the negative consequences of failing to adopt the change. This is a style that people may find threatening.

Push back or resistance is a typical response to *push,* particularly when a moderate or higher degree is employed.

A *push* strategy is usually high energy and short-term because people are constrained to change and the process will lose all momentum as soon as the *push* stops.

Employing a strong *push* may be appropriate in a crisis/survival situation, when speed is of the essence, but you should *always* start with the lowest level of *push.*

If you are *all powerful* (see Figure 2.2) then a strong *push* can be effective to accelerate change. However, such behaviour may be seen as heavy handed or even aggressive, which can have negative consequences that last for a very long time after the *push.*

Leading Change Using Pull

Using a *pull* approach aims to reduce resistance to change and engaging people in such a way that they want to comply willingly. There are three degrees of *pull* that the change leader will move through *during* the change process.

The lowest entry level *pull* involves the change leader listening to the affected group and endeavouring to understand their position. This requires honesty and openness and a disclosure of true feelings to help develop trust. It may be necessary for the change leader to adapt their influencing style/personality and to lead by example. By better understanding those affected, the change leader is more able to identify mutual goals which enable them to see what's in it for them. The focus is on lowering resistance.

The next level of *pull* implies the change leader employing motivators to alter the view of change of those affected. The aim is to achieve a shared vision by exploring possibilities, taking time to explain the *why* and *how* and identifying benefits for all. Enthusiasm, encouragement, thanks and praise are the key leadership behaviours at this level.

At the highest level of *pull*, the change leader gives ownership for change to those affected. At this point those affected take responsibility for and start to solve the problems for themselves. As they become committed to the change the leader should offer both recognition and praise.

The *pull* approach aims for a Win/Win and requires significant effort by the change leader from the start to get to really know those affected. When this approach is adopted people will tend to want to change and the transformation will continue after the *pull* has stopped.

Addressing People's Needs

Understanding people's style will help the change leader to engage effectively with those affected. But, as the *pull* approach suggests the leader also requires an understanding of different people's needs, if they are to be motivated to support the change. Applying Maslow's hierarchy (Figure 2.4) can help to identify the options a change leader might propose.

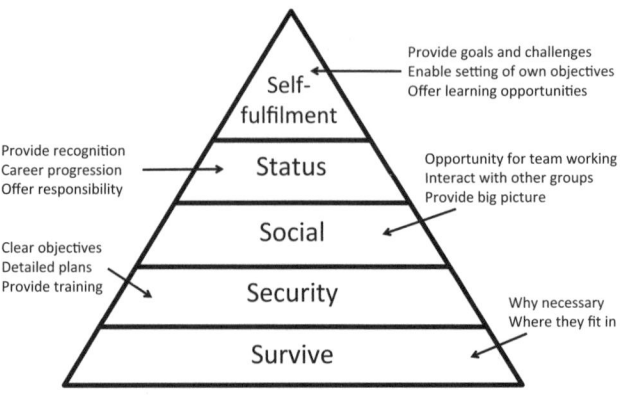

Figure 2.4   Applying Maslow's Hierarchy

When introducing a change people will often worry:

- whether they will have a job in the immediate future;

- whether they will have the skills to cope, both during and after the change;

- who they will be working with in the future;

- about losing their status;

- about the enormity of the challenge ahead.

The position an individual occupies in the hierarchy will determine the actions the change leader needs to take whilst managing the change. Figure 2.4 provides a few examples of the actions a change leader might take for each level in the hierarchy. For example for the majority of the workforce the change leader's actions may mainly focus on the *survive, security* and *social* aspects, but for managers/team leaders and more senior staff attention should also be paid to *status* and *self-fulfilment*.

Always remember that key individuals/opinion formers reside at all levels in the organization. Their *status* and *self-fulfilment* needs, where present, also need to be addressed, if their support for the change is to be enlisted.

Key Player(s) Planning

Having identified who are the major players, recognized their influencing style and determined how they might be engaged, you can now develop a plan. Once you have determined their attitude/commitment to the proposed change (Figure 2.2), the next step is to consider the power and authority they have within the organization. Figure 2.5 indicates some ideas that you might adopt when determining the change strategy.

High	Find an incentive to support you or distract and isolate them from the project	Find an incentive to support change and look for opportunity to involve them	Nurture and actively involve them in the change
Medium	Find an incentive to support you or distract and isolate them from the project	Find an incentive to support change and look for opportunity to involve them	Build an alliance
Low	Leave alone	Leave alone, but occasionally check to see if attitude changes	Build an alliance
	Against	**Neutral Attitude**	**For**

Figure 2.5 **Power and Influence**

Exercise 11

Draw a planning matrix and using the information obtained in Exercise 10, plot the positions of key players within the matrix. Develop strategies to help you obtain the maximum support for your change. Remember that the best strategies are usually ones that take a *pull* approach to influencing.

Managing the Change

Successful organizational transformation not only requires visionary leadership, but also needs exceptional management skills. It is unlikely that the change leader can do everything themselves, and so they must assemble an energetic and committed team who will help both to lead and manage the change programme.

Robust programme and project management frameworks, tools and techniques should be employed to ensure the transformation is managed appropriately.

There are several key questions concerning purpose, structure, incentives, supporting mechanisms, relationships and management that need to be asked by the leadership team before the change programme implementation commences.

Answering the questions about *key success factors* posed in Figure 2.6, will help identify any gaps before the programme is launched.

Exercise 12

Complete the Key Success Factors Table (Figure 2.6).

Starting with the factor that has the lowest score, develop a series of action plans that will make it excellent.

How to Spot When it is Going Wrong!

Whenever there is pressure to change there is an associated resistance that endeavours to maintain the status quo. If the change agent is perceived to lack the authority and/or credibility to lead the changes then the following series of *resisting behaviours* (intimidation rituals) are likely to be observed.

- Nullification;
- Isolation;
- Defamation;
- Expulsion.

These behaviours will increase in their severity and start with covert intimidation.

Key Success Factors	Non existent 0	1	2	3	4	5	6	7	8	Excellent 9
Purpose										
Clear objective										
Common vision										
Structure										
Key roles/people identified										
Projects identified										
Resources identified										
Incentives										
Rewards support changes										
Key tasks have incentives										
Helpful Mechanisms										
Communication plan										
Systems support change										
Project management skills										
Education/training programme										
Relationships										
United leadership team										
Those affected involved										
Issues allowed to surface										
Conflict resolution plan										
People support plans										
Management										
Programme management										
Responsibilities assigned										

Figure 2.6   Key Success Factors

Nullification

Initially resistance will take the form of nullification; statements like: "You are new here and do not understand the culture."

Isolation

If you persist with your actions the resisting forces will then try to isolate you from the rest of the organization and soften the impact of your reforms. This may take the form of not inviting you to meetings or missing you off distribution lists and so on.

If you persist in the change the pressure increases with direct intimidation, which takes the form of the next level which is defamation.

Defamation

Impugning your character to cut you off from any support you might have, for example, by questioning your motives for pursuing the change.

Expulsion

If you do not voluntarily abandon your actions the final ritual is to expel you. This not only prevents you from introducing change, but also serves as a warning to other would-be reformers.

To avoid these rituals it is of paramount importance that you possess adequate credibility/authority to lead the change and that you clarify and agree everybody's roles and expectations from the outset.

Strategies for Handling Difficult People

Below are a few strategies for managing influential problem people.

Vocal

*   Avoid large meetings – they love an audience.

*   Involve early.

*   Put them in charge of something – but maintain a firm grip.

*   Load what they are doing for success.

*   Once successful enlist them as an ally.

Yes, but …, been there, seen it before

*   Enlist help.

*   Ask for a list of potential problems, then

*   Ask for a list of solutions from them.

There is a devious reason for this …

*   Explain, if possible, the *why* and *what* behind the plan.

*   Offer them an organizing role.

*   Keep a close eye on what they do.

In agreement, but will not publicly say so

*   Encourage small group discussions with like-minded people.

*   Keep them apart from influential opponents.

*   Do a pilot in their area – load for success.

Achieving lasting VICTORY – hints and tips

Successful change leadership is all about getting the organization initially to start thinking about change and preparing for change, and then making and sustaining the change. To achieve VICTORY, change leaders should ensure there is:

Vision: To transform the paper strategies into a way of life. Vision empowers people to change and should play a central role in their life. If people share the vision there is likely to be:

- Ownership;
- Commitment;
- Drive;
- Energy;
- Excitement;
- Innovation;
- Self-management.

Inclusion: People affected by the change need to be involved:

- Inform those likely to be affected early.
- Involve people in designing the change and the new ways of working.

Remember:

- You never get a second chance to involve people from the start.
- Once someone has been cut out, they feel alienated.

Communications: Effective communication throughout the change is vital, it should be a dialogue and:

- Must be planned.
- Must be more credible than the rumours.
- Has to be early and ongoing.
- Must be encouraged.
- Needs to respond immediately to key queries and concerns.
- People affected by the change need to have a chance to express their feelings about it – without fear of reprisals.

Timing: The timing of key interventions, particularly the early ones, is often crucial to success:

- Do not work blind.

- Work with the responsive – friends and allies initially.

- Start in the most promising areas.

- Load individual projects for success – particularly the early ones.

- Stop digging when you are in a hole.

Organization: Spend time organizing the key people and planning for the change:

- Assemble a group with enough power to lead the change effort.

- Identify the key (influential) individuals/groups affected and take time to understand their position/view.

- Develop strategies for achieving your vision.

- Develop top level programme and project plans that may be passed to the implementation teams.

Resistance reduced: It is normal for people to resist change. But there are many things a leader can do that can help reduce resistance and establish some momentum:

- Select positive people to run projects.

- Provide valid information and explain reasons.

- Avoid coercion and treat everybody honourably.

- Share decision-making – listen and get reaction.

- Do not over-react to the feedback.

- Sell the benefits but do not over-sell.

- Minimize social change.

- Reward those who change, particularly the trailblazers.

- Review and if necessary modify the approach on the basis of what you learn.

You: Take care of yourself, so that you have the vigour to see the vision through. If you do not wish to become an early casualty remember that as leader:

- Your credibility is the currency that funds the change.

- You will have to invest significant amounts of both your energy and personal credibility to inspire action and deliver worthwhile results.

- You will be *known* by your words at the beginning. But very soon you will be *judged* by your deeds.

- You are unlikely to be able to do everything yourself and you must delegate to capable people.

- You must keep an eye on the organization's politics, particularly the *realpolitik* of balancing your rhetoric with action to increase your credibility continually.

Chapters 1 and 2 have provided some theory tools and techniques that can help change leaders increase the likelihood of success. Once most of the approaches have been used a few times they will become second nature, always remembering that, *"Leadership is personal, a relationship with credibility at the cornerstone."*

Chapter 3 of this book assembles many of the ideas discussed throughout the text into a set of activities, based around FEE and LIPS concepts and a step-by-step approach to organizational transformation.

3 75 Ways to Help Sustain Organizational Transformation

This chapter contains a compendium of 75 actions that you may take to promote and sustain transformation within your organization. The activities are grouped under their most relevant FEE and LIPS heading, although a number are interlinked and will have an influence across more than one category.

INVESTING FOR FUTURE TRANSFORMATION – PAYING THE FEE

There are many activities that an organization's leadership may invest in to lay the foundation for future ongoing transformation. The initial activities should be around developing and maintaining an underlying culture of empowerment, one in which learning and change are celebrated. As well as people development activities you will need to modify the policies, procedures and processes that underpin the organization. Management rhetoric must be matched by action. Over the years I have discovered that the quick test to discover whether an organization has developed an underlying transformation culture is to ask people outright. Those that have such a culture are only too ready to invite you both to discuss their approach to change and demonstrate how they operate. Not only do they *walk the talk*, they also *talk the walk*. The 29 items covered by this section identify some of the activities we can undertake to lay the foundations for continuous organizational transformation.

Feelings

1. Minimize surprises
If our managers are continually surprising us we will become increasingly uncertain and uneasy. We spend considerable time and effort involving ourselves with the latest rumour rather than being productive and continual uncertainty may lead us to seek alternative employment.

To help prepare for the unexpected, the leadership team can undertake a series of scenario planning exercises that cover a range of shock situations. In this way there are plans in place to manage surprise. However, although planning is an important element, a robust internal communication process is critical to manage these situations successfully.

Of course there will be times when the organizations cannot avoid shocks or surprises. By having a robust communication process coupled with positive direction from the leadership team and well-rehearsed responses, the change-sustaining organization is able to manage these surprises and minimize the impact on staff feelings and performance.

2. Empower and encourage staff

An underlying culture of encouragement and empowerment helps us to feel valued, supported and to also have a high degree of control/discretion over our daily activities. We will have positive feelings if we understand the plan, where we fit into it, the scope and boundaries to our role and how we will be supported.

This allows frontline staff to respond to changing situations without constantly seeking advice from the centre. This enables the leadership team to concentrate on the overall strategy and not be distracted by disturbances at the fringes.

3. Respect staff professionalism

This is an extension of empowerment. We feel good about the organization if we believe that the skill, knowledge and experience we bring to bear in our role, that is our professionalism, is respected by our managers and leaders.

The leadership team needs to convey this continually, in their words and actions to ensure that people's skill, knowledge and experience are developed and rewarded.

4. Create openness

This too is a cultural aspect. Do people in your organization speak their mind or are the messages they communicate coded or diluted in the hope they are more palatable to the recipient. Are we doing it for them or for ourselves? It is usually the latter. Introducing a spirit of openness starts at the top of the organization.

How the leaders are seen to behave will have a profound influence on communication throughout the organization. Open communication requires high levels of trust that, once established, provide powerful support to our feelings towards the organization and its leadership.

5. Avoid creating losers

When continual change becomes the norm, then how the organization treats those people that are unwilling/unable to change, or are no longer required, will have a profound influence on those who remain. Avoid creating individuals or groups who can be perceived as an underclass, as people will fear that they may end up in that category. Fear, particularly the fear of failure, is a very powerful resistor.

6. Treat those who are leaving honourably

Every effort must be made and be seen to be made both to convince, help and support the unwilling and unable categories. If, at the end of the day, staff are required to leave, for whatever reason, they must be allowed to do so honourably.

The change-sustaining organization will have change policies and procedures that address staff support and how people may exit the organization with dignity.

Experience

7. Check you are ready

Before any explorer embarks on an expedition they will ensure they have appropriate resources available both for the journey and for coping with the unexpected.

Develop methods/techniques to assess that the organization is ready for change. An extension of the annual attitude survey can provide some general information, but why not take a leaf from the military and conduct some exercises to show how parts of the organization respond. For example, we do not allow a new submarine to go off on patrol until its systems, crew and leaders have been tried and tested. Develop your own assessment methods to ensure your organization is ready to cast off.

8. Start filling the gaps

If you are assessing your readiness then you must have in place the strategies and processes for filling any skill, knowledge and experience gaps you have identified. Do not wait until a problem is encountered, develop the process and test it.

9. Prime change with external resources

Organizational inertia can mean that change often needs a kick-start to get things moving. You may require new and additional skills or extra bodies to help spread the message and/or support some sections of the organization to get rolling. These skills are rarely cheap and if they appear to be so, critically examine just what you are receiving for your money. A clear and tight contract is key, or it can become expensive in the longer term. A builder I knew won a great deal of profitable work by bidding the lowest price and then encouraging the client to require extras (many of which were contained in his competitors' price) that were extremely expensive.

10. But do not become dependent

That same builder was expert at remaining at his clients' properties for weeks or months after the original piece of work had been completed. He would constantly find other things that needed attention and offer to fix them. Soon he would be tackling jobs that the householder would normally undertake and be well paid for it.

In the organizational context, use external resources to support the change, but always see them as a temporary expedient. Avoid scope creep and ensure you have a clear contract.

11. Insist on skill and knowledge transfer

You should avoid becoming dependent on these external resources, particularly if they are providing expert knowledge. At the start of this book it was suggested that change was the only constant and the successful organizations need to be continually changing. Having the skills for continual transformation is a necessary core competence that in the long-term should not be outsourced to a third party.

Make it a contractual condition on external resource providers that a key element of their assignment is the transfer of their skill and knowledge to your organization. In this way you will be learning to do it for yourself and the skills acquired may be of benefit beyond the original change project. However, this does not necessarily mean that you would use these types of resource only once. If consultants are really good at their job they will be finding new and better ways of doing things and you will wish to employ on future projects. Never pay for the same experience twice, always seek more value.

12. Develop an in-house change capability

It is futile to insist on skill and knowledge transfer, unless you have a mechanism for accepting the transfer. This in turn requires the development of an in-house change capability. Developing such a capability requires attention to both the people and process aspects. The first stage is to select a person or persons who themselves have good consultancy skills and are both inquisitive and enthusiastic about new things. You then need to give them some space and time to work out how best they can learn, capture and then retain knowledge for the organization's future use. Software tools may be introduced to assist with this activity, as may the rotation of staff through a change unit or some such organizational entity. The style and structure will need to be in line with what the organization is trying to be, not what it currently is.

13. Get smarter each time you change

Getting smarter is all about doing things quicker and easier. It involves the application of the learning and knowledge that has been acquired during a change process.

When embarking on a major change programme spend some time reviewing the early phases so that the experience, knowledge and capabilities that have been acquired at the start can be deployed smartly during the later phases.

14. Learn from your customers

Make sure that whatever you offer to your customers gets better every time they use it. Achieve this by building a feedback loop into your offer so that it automatically teaches you to do things better next time. If you are continually learning from your customers then you will be continuously changing rather than playing an annual game of catch up.

15. Develop your people

People development must be a key constituent of any change strategy as simply learning during the change will be insufficient to ensure its success.

People development is the proactive leadership element of a continuous learning philosophy. Spend time exploring and understanding what the new world will be like and the necessary skills that are needed to succeed. Produce an organization-wide learning plan that demonstrates how those affected will acquire the skills they require for the future.

16. Develop tools

Some time ago I saw a list of the relative efficiency of different species in expending energy when getting from A to B. The condor was found to be the most efficient, with humans well down the list. However, if you put a human on a bicycle, they then become twice as efficient as the condor. Developing tools to assist us achieve our goal has been a feature of human beings for approaching two million years.

When embarking on a change programme start by investigating what tools can be developed to increase the efficiency of people going through the change. It may be tools to help them with their new tasks or it may be events that will help them cope with the change.

Environment

17. Adopt a continuous learning philosophy

Adopting a continuous learning philosophy makes it easier to get smarter no matter what the organization is doing.

Having successfully instituted some learning processes at the start of the change programme so you can become smarter; expand the concept to all aspects of organization. The small learning steps you achieved in getting smarter will assist in selling the concept and developing the philosophy and processes throughout the organization. Treat learning as a project within the overall change programme.

18. Prize your intellectual assets

Think of your intellectual assets as the organization's crown jewels and treat them in a similar way.

Using the crown jewel metaphor the organization must develop processes and procedures to add continually to the collection and protect them from theft and decay. Most importantly make them available for all to see and highlight their importance in the organization's rituals and celebrations.

19. Treat change as an opportunity

One of the quickest ways through the denial phase is to look actively for the opportunities that change has presented, rather than what is going to be lost. Develop your creative and innovative skills to explore and exploit the new situation that has been presented to you.

20. Organize and fund the business to respond quickly

Review your current structure, systems and processes and investigate how they can be reconfigured for greater flexibility and responsiveness. Start by developing analogies based on, for example, how nature or the military organizes for and responds to unexpected situations. Invest in developing systems that can support change – make it part of the selection criteria.

21. Have systems and procedures to manage risks

To paraphrase Machiavelli – *There is nothing so uncertain or risky as undertaking organizational change*. When we embark upon a change our strategy will have been based on any number of assumptions. These must be captured, documented, assessed for impact and likelihood, and plans put in place to manage those that are likely to affect the desired outcome.

22. Make speed of management action key

Foster speed and directness of management action. Develop systems and processes to provide information to the organization's managers quickly and develop these managers to make incisive decisions based on imperfect information. Beware of punishing mistakes and encourage them to learn from the experience.

23. Help your customers to get smarter

Use your product/service offering to help your customers learn more about your organization and getting the best from it. The smarter they are the easier it becomes to engage with them to change/develop the offer. This is particularly true as many products now also contain service elements. How can your smart customer help you introduce the desired change most effectively?

24. Help your suppliers to get smarter

Encourage your customers to adopt idea 23 with their customers too. You want any changes they make to be to your advantage.

25. Find partners

Undertaking major change, particularly when it is industry-wide is very risky. In the aircraft industry European manufacturers formed a consortium, Airbus Industries, to design and build aircraft to rival the US manufacturers. It is unlikely that any of the consortium members had the financial strength to undertake such a project alone and, even if they had, their potential customers would perceive it as a high risk undertaking and be less inclined to purchase such an aircraft, no matter how good. When there is significant environmental change check to see if there are suppliers, customers or competitors with whom you might partner. It can produce a lot more opportunities at a lot less risk to the individuals.

41

26. Continually remove the fences and fill ditches

The three key words when undertaking change are Preparation, Preparation and Preparation! Every organization has (some) barriers to change. They may even be the last series of successful changes. Work continually to identify the barriers and prepare the ground in advance of launching the programme. The fences and ditches can rapidly slow progress and nothing demoralizes the organization quicker than when it becomes bogged down early on in the change.

27. Be big and small

What is the right size for your organization? You need to be small enough to respond nimbly to change, yet big enough to behave as a global player. If you are a large corporation then you will need to disaggregate yourself into smaller work units and, if you are a small organization, you will need to link yourself to others to demonstrate strength and depth. Being electronically connected is the key, so you can appear and behave as both big and small simultaneously.

28. Learn to adapt continually

Continual adaptation requires you be in tune with your environment. Let the external market signals determine how you should be organized rather than management dictate. Leadership, having set the course, should not keep a dead hand on the tiller, particularly if a powerful headwind has sprung up, but rather allow the organization to tack as appropriate.

29. Regularly review the strategic management process

The key management process of translating the vision to action should be one of the most stimulating and purposeful activities in which the leadership team are involved.

Regularly check your process to assess how well it serves to:

- Build a realistic vision of the future.

- Commit senior management to action plans to achieve the vision.

- Identify customer and technological opportunities on a continuous basis.

- Develop the leadership team and key support members of the organization.

- Provide a sense of direction and framework to evaluate product/ service strategies.

- Adapt the organization to changes in the market.

- Create a common sense of purpose to drive the organization forward.

- Develop the necessary corporate culture.

MOVING THE ORGANIZATION FORWARD – USING YOUR LIPS

In the first section of this chapter we have considered how people need to be prepared for change, so they are receptive, rather than resistant, to organizational transformation initiatives. Once the organization is in a receptive state its people can then be motivated to change. It should be of no surprise to the reader that almost 50 per cent of the remaining items come under the heading of leadership, the cornerstone of all successful transformations. But leadership alone will not achieve the organization's goals. It must be supported by incentives, plans and by making people feel not only included, but also actively involved in the change. During the early stages of transformation the change leader often needs to act as an umbrella to the organization, protecting it from hostile elements whilst the necessary transformation culture, along with its supporting processes and structures, is fostered and developed. That said, the following items focus on the types of activity necessary to achieve ongoing organizational transformation.

Leadership

30. Be ambitious, audacious and strategic

People who make a real difference are usually driven. They will have a personal agenda be it fame, fortune or a combination of the two. But, personal ambition to succeed is not enough; you also need to be audacious and courageous in the way you lead. Books, the internet and other media provide many insights into what drove great leaders, be they politicians, religious, military or business leaders. Only appoint a change leader who sees it as an opportunity to develop and progress themselves as well as the organization. Transformation success also requires a strong strategic focus with any transformation closely linked to a robust business strategy.

31. Articulate the vision and have a consistent message

Moses, the first recorded change leader, was not good with words. He recognized that if he were to convince the Israelites to leave Egypt then he needed to enlist the help of Aaron to manage the communications and public relations aspects of the change.

As change leader you may need to articulate the vision in a number of languages for the different levels and sections of the organization. It must be a consistent message, but presented in such a way that it is meaningful to the recipient. If so called one-size T-shirts rarely fit anybody well, why expect one change message to suit all?

32. Enlist support from the senior team

Change leaders cannot do everything themselves, or burn-out will occur before the programme is halfway complete. The senior team must actively support both the leader and the programme. And support means exactly what it says, take some of the load. If they are seen to be actively involved then it is more likely that the rest of the organization will follow.

If senior team members feel unable to support the initiative, the leader has the three "R" options, to Resign, to Rethink or to Relieve appropriate senior team members of their duties – avoiding creating martyrs.

33. Develop a real sense of urgency and mission

Having examined the market and competitive realities, identify the crisis/opportunity and discuss it openly throughout the organization. Give people a chance to grasp the reality of the situation and then provide a clear way forward that addresses these issues.

34. Allow people time

Think back to the dip curve (Figure 1.4) in Chapter 1. We need time to become accustomed to change. How long it takes will depend on the severity of the change, the activities undertaken to support staff going through it, as well as individual personal circumstances.

Introduce activities that help people to celebrate the past and look forward to the future. Always remember that senior members of the organization probably knew about the change some time before the rank and file, so they are likely to be in advance of them. If they feel any frustration because the organization is lagging they should avoid showing it, but instead find new and creative ways to help everybody else move forward.

35. But not too much time

This may appear to be a contradiction to item 34, but waiting for the rest of the organization to get moving may be a form of creative avoidance. You need to change your thinking about time by aiming to reduce the time it takes to do something by a third each time you repeat the exercise. If your last major organizational change took 18 months to implement, plan to do it in 12 months next time and eight months the time after that. You will need to be both creative and innovative in your approach and probably employ a fair amount of technology to provide both support and flexibility. But, given that today's organization has to constantly change within three years, you'll be able to introduce a major change within three months.

36. Select tough but achievable goals

Easy goals will not bring about sustainable change, as they will not be perceived by the organization as likely to make a difference and people will not bother. Impossible goals (or those that are perceived as impossible) will result in people not trying or rapidly becoming demoralized and giving up. A smart leader will set a series of goals that get tougher along the way. In this way their people will be stretched and developed in exactly the same way that athletes might develop themselves when they set out to break a record.

Athletics provides some wonderful metaphors around change. Spend a few moments thinking about the similarities and differences between developing an athlete and changing an organization.

37. Establish a fully inclusive communications programme

Use every vehicle possible to communicate the new vision and strategies. Include all levels in the organization and provide them with the opportunity to feed back their thoughts and ideas. Introduce processes and procedures that will facilitate an ongoing change dialogue with the whole organization.

38. Clearly establish project sponsor and management roles

There are likely to be a number of discrete projects that make up a change programme. Each project should have a sponsor and project manager, the former will be a senior executive who initiates it and is accountable for its outcome, with the latter being responsible for achieving the project's objectives and leading the project team. Time should be taken to ensure there is clarity of both purpose and responsibilities.

39. Create a change programme champion

Change champions must come from the highest levels of the organization. The champion should head a coalition of senior executives, encouraging them to work together as a team and providing a clear figurehead for the rest of the organization to rally round.

40. Continually demonstrate the leadership's commitment

It often does not take long for a change initiative's momentum to slow. One metaphor I like to use is that the change leadership team has to operate like jugglers who have to keep a large number of plates spinning on the tops of bamboo canes. Demonstrating their continual commitment is the equivalent of the juggler giving the canes a twist. Failure to do so will result in projects, like the metaphorical plates, coming crashing down.

41. Ensure the leaders are regularly out in the organization

See and be seen is the watchword. Leaders who are regularly out in the organization soon get a sense for what is really happening. They have a feel for things before the monthly figures hit their desk – these should just provide confirmation to the leaders' intuition. Being seen is also reassuring for the rest of the organization, management are not perceived as remote and leadership is interested in their everyday activities. Such an approach will also facilitate the organization's all important change dialogue.

42. Grow and develop leaders throughout the organization

Successful organizations that have survived over the long-term, for example, IBM, not only work at understanding their current and future competency requirements, but also trawl their staff to identify future senior managers and executives who are then developed and coached appropriately.

43. Lead your customers

Do not just tell your key customers about your change programme, get them actively involved in its realization. Lead joint workshops/activities aimed at helping them understand your goals and how you can assist each other in the future.

44. Lead your suppliers

Do the same for your key suppliers.

45. Lead your shareholders

Not forgetting the shareholders. You do not want them to become nervous halfway through your programme. Engage them early and keep them informed every step of the way ensuring that your counter-rumour processes and procedures are always ready for action.

46. Avoid maturity

Initiate change before the "S" curve flattens. You often need extra funds to drive change, something that slow growth rates and diminishing margins are unlikely to provide.

45

47. Always look for new opportunities

The previous item indicates that smart organizations will tend to exit more quickly from declining markets. However, you need to know in which direction to move or it could be a case of *out of the frying pan and into the fire*. Armed with a vision of your long-term future you can scan the emerging trends continuously to identify the business opportunities for you to exploit with early market entry. How the organization responds to new opportunities is a good measure of how effective it is at managing change.

48. Make your requirements of everybody explicit

Anything that is not explicit will be more open to misinterpretation. The greater the degree of interpretation the less likelihood of achieving a sustainable change programme.

49. Communicate with the organization continuously

Appoint a senior member of the leadership team to be accountable for successful communications. Use all media to conduct your continuing dialogue. Even when there is nothing new, reassure everybody there is nothing new to report. Actively listen to observations and comments from both within and without the organization.

50. Consider how to employ emerging technologies

Invest in time to research new technologies from both a tactical and strategic standpoint across all dimensions of the business: examples of this include distribution technology, learning technology, promotion technology and so on, not forgetting information technology. Develop a technology audit framework so you can identify where you lead or lag, together with the associated outcomes.

Incentives

51. Ensure change is seen as essential

Chapter 1 of this book indicated how humans deny or ignore that change is needed or is occurring.

To get the organization to move along your chosen path, you must clearly demonstrate the advantages of the end-state. But in some instances ...

52. A little pain can help

You may remember the Bible story of how both the Egyptians and Israelites needed to experience a number of plagues before either would act. Some chief executives have been known to engineer a crisis to bring the need for change into sharp focus.

53. Use your best people

Using your best people demonstrates to the rest of the organization that this project is very important. This one act can create a change positive environment and encourage others to be up for it.

54. Reward all staff for embracing change

Reward staff as they adopt the changes. The reward need not be financial – although it can help; it may be a visit from the president, chairman or CEO, a mention in the company newsletter or a coffee mug and desktop trivia that celebrates the new.

55. Be especially sure to reward the trailblazers

Trailblazing and being an early adopter of a change can be very risky for those individuals concerned as they risk the alienation of their peers. Providing some reward for their behaviour can work as both a thank you to those who have progressed and an encouragement for those yet to make the transition.

Plans

56. Divide a major change into manageable steps

Question: "How do you eat an elephant?" Answer: "One slice at a time." The act of slicing up your complex change project will help people to understand how do-able it is. The unskilled change leader will describe complexity in terms of barriers to success. The skilled change leader will simplify complexity, emphasizing how manageable the change is.

57. Assess the benefits before starting

The vision must be grounded in quantifiable benefits before the journey commences. In this way cost/benefit milestones may be set to enable good management every step of the way. Throughout the change "What gets measured, gets done" must be the key maxim, and understanding and quantifying the benefits will help ensure appropriate metrics are in place.

58. Identify allies

Identifying allies for implementing the critical early phases of the programme will often be crucial to overall success. Not only will they help ensure the initial projects succeed, but they will also be advocates for moving the programme onto its subsequent phases.

59. Test to find the most promising propositions

The environment within which you are running your change programme will also be in a state of flux and the original plan can very quickly become sub-optimal. Throughout the life of the programme it will be necessary to conduct ongoing research, so you can modify the implementation to enable you continually to select the lowest risk and highest return options.

60. Clearly define roles and responsibilities

Be RACI when planning. For each programme or project activity define:

- who is **R**esponsible for undertaking the work;

- who is **A**ccountable for its outcome;

- who needs to be **C**onsulted or provide support; and

- who should be kept **I**nformed.[1]

61. Start with a small step

Do not be over ambitious when launching the programme. Start with a manageable step and learn as much as you can from it before taking the next one. Each subsequent step should increasingly stretch the organization, with success becoming the natural order of things.

62. Load early projects for success

Take a leaf from the military tactician's book. Ensure you have massively superior resources at your command when you initiate the break-out from the current situation.

If necessary supplement your resources with external support – subject to the usual caveat of learning from them. To ensure there is sufficient leverage you may have to reduce resources elsewhere within the organization to a minimum. Only after you have established a bridgehead and achieved a good momentum behind the programme can these additional resources be redeployed.

63. Use the early adopters

Wherever possible use the early adopters as ambassadors for change. Living examples of success are worth a thousand reports of success.

64. Slay sacred cows

Sacred cows make great steaks. All plans should include the identification and culling of these beasts! No business process should be sacrosanct.

65. Plan to learn from mistakes

It is extremely rare for a complex change programme to go according to plan. You need to acknowledge that mistakes will be made and design for appropriate allowances in your plans. However, it is unacceptable for the same mistake to be made continually. Create a register to capture errors/issues and introduce a process so they are reviewed and the learning both captured and appropriately disseminated to minimize the likelihood of a further occurrence.

---

1   The RACI idea is expanded in Chapter 4 with the suggestion that people who need to be activity managed should also be identified.

66. Check benefits were achieved

At the end of the programme, review what benefits have been achieved and how they compare to the ones stated at the programme launch, investigating and learning from the variances. But do not wait until the end of the programme. Set and review regular milestones to track the likelihood of benefit achievement.

Sense of Involvement

67. Check goal validity with key stakeholders

The key stakeholders for every phase/project of the programme will have been identified during the preliminary planning stage. Check the goals before commencing detailed planning and again at the start of each implementation project. Keep them informed during their project's life and review achievement following its completion. Their involvement can ensure you have useful allies during a project and powerful advocates in support of subsequent phases of the programme.

68. Always involve the affected group

Provide some latitude for modification in the implementation, so that the affected group can contribute to its final design and make it their plan rather than your plan. At the end of the change you want them to say, "We did this" not "This was done to us".

69. Use a cross-functional approach

Creating a cross-function project team will have a number of significant benefits, with the increased likelihood of:

- A wider set of skills.

- Different experiences and approaches.

- Challenging current perceived best practice.

- Learning from each other.

- A positive approach, if one or more of the team are from areas that have already had a successful implementation.

70. Seconding key people

The action of seconding key people to projects clearly demonstrates that you believe this programme is important. They are also likely to inspire their team and the affected group.

71. Involve the support functions

Involve the organization's support functions such as Human Resources and Information Technology right from the start. They may bring a different perspective to the proposed transition and are certainly needed for their knowledge of personnel law, training and competence development nor would you wish your transition to founder on the rocks of inappropriate or incompatible technologies.

72. Establish change teams to drive the project activities

Establish change teams that report into the leadership team. These teams, typically led by the transition programme director (a senior leadership team member) will be empowered to deliver the programme through their individual projects. Empowerment requires them to be provided with their project goals and boundaries allowing them the scope to plan and implement in the most appropriate manner.

73. Have a rapid and consistent mechanism for cascading goals

Ensure there is a process, such as Balanced Scorecard, in place that helps you to convert corporate goals to division goals and so on down to individual goals. When people understand what is in it for them and how they fit in, then you have a higher probability that everybody will start pulling in the same direction.

74. And include a feedback mechanism

Cascade provides a powerful metaphor for rapid unidirectional process – like a succession of waterfalls. Whilst cascade velocity is important it is also necessary to rapidly feed back any issues and concerns about the goals. Often this is due to a lack of goal clarity and misunderstanding, but it can be that some goals have become mutually inconsistent during the process and these will require rapid resolution.

75. Devolve as much as possible

It is all too easy for change leaders to take everything upon themselves, this might work in the short run, but in the longer term the leader and their programme are likely to run out of steam. Leaders should devolve as much of the implementation as possible. In this way they are able to concentrate on the overall transition strategy, provide highly visible leadership and focus all of their energy on resolving critical issues that may kill the transition. Devolving also requires the involvement of others and the more people who are actively involved in the transformation process the greater the chance of its success.

WHAT NEXT?

The 75 suggestions that you have been given are a beginning, and following the suggestion in Chapter 1, you may well have already added to them. Whenever I am asked, "So where do you start?" I always answer with "Start where your and the organization's energy is most apparent and start with a small step." Remember that although the previous two sections have been laid out as 75 discrete activities, many of them are interrelated, some weakly and others much more strongly so when you undertake one you can often positively influence others.

An excellent place to start is with the Environment set, which have a strong emphasis on the underlying organizational culture and processes. Remember that as soon as you commence this activity you have initiated a change programme and therefore you will need to apply some of the principles of FEE and LIPS immediately. In these early stages it is important to maintain a balance between growing your own change capabilities and developing your strategic intent. In any event, spend time understanding this first project's environment, enlist support of your allies, start with a small step and load it for success.

Some people like to work sequentially and Figure 3.1 provides an outline progression of steps that would underpin an organizational transformation, together with where each one of the 75 Ways is most applicable. However, we must be careful not to think of a transformation being a simple linear process. In some instances the steps will overlap and many of the 75 Ways are appropriate at more than one step and some, particularly the resistors, are applicable throughout such an exercise.

Step Description	Examples of Typical Activities	Most Applicable Ways
Understanding your position and creating a sense of urgency	Environment scanning. Examining market and competitive realities. Identifying potential opportunities and crises.	7, 18, 19, 25, 29, 46, 50, 59,
Forming a powerful team for change	Reviewing capabilities. Assembling a group of people with enough energy and commitment to lead the change. Encouraging them to work together as a team.	32, 38, 39
Constructing the vision	Developing a vision that will help focus the organization for action. Developing strategies for achieving the vision.	30, 33, 51, 52
Communicating the vision and listening	Communicate the vision and strategies using every method possible. The change team are an example of the organization's new behaviours.	1, 31, 34, 35, 37, 40, 41
Empowering the organization to act on the vision	Encouraging staff to work in new ways. Removing obstacles to change. Changing processes and structures that suppress the vision.	2, 3, 4, 12, 14, 15, 16, 17, 42, 48, 67, 75
Planning and delivering quick wins	Identifying key opportunities. Planning improvements. Delivering the improvements. Recognizing and rewarding staff involved in achieving the improvements.	9, 10, 11, 53, 54, 55, 56, 57, 58, 59, 60, 61, 62
Consolidating the improvements	Systematically progress through the organization changing policies, systems and structures that do not fit the vision. Develop staff who can implement the vision.	5, 6, 8, 13, 20, 21, 22, 47, 63, 64, 65, 66, 70, 71, 72, 73, 74
Embed the new approaches	Continually demonstrate the connections between the new approaches and success. Develop all stakeholders. Ensure succession of change leadership.	23, 24, 26, 27, 28, 43, 44, 45, 68, 69

Figure 3.1   Activities for Overcoming Resistance

4 Implementation: Successfully Managing the Change Project

INTRODUCTION

In the first three chapters of this book the focus was on Change Leadership. But successful organizational change also requires discipline and the application of good management techniques. As explained earlier, good planning, checking on progress and capturing the learning are key to introducing successful change and developing an organization's capabilities. The aim of this chapter is to assist the change leader appreciate the main aspects of managing successful change projects. The change leader is unlikely to undertake all the activities discussed themselves, but will often delegate much of the day-to-day running of the change project to another member of their team. However, the skills and techniques examined in this chapter are still valuable in any management role. To help the change leader, this chapter will examine:

- The nature of projects.

- Project planning.

- Implementing the plan to the project's successful conclusion.

By doing this the change leader will provide a structured approach to project management so that they may ensure the range of appropriate skills are brought together so as to load their change project for success. There is a *Suggested Further Reading* at the end of the book so those who are interested may delve deeper into the subject. The most important step the change leader or sponsor should do is recruit a good project manager to manage the change as the leader will not be able to undertake both roles by themselves. But what the leader should have is an excellent appreciation of how your project manager goes about their tasks. This appreciation will enable the change leader to ask the right question so you remain confident that your vision remains on track.

When you first start using the tools, techniques and processes mentioned in the book they will probably feel a little strange or awkward, just as when learning to ride a bike. It may take a little while to feel comfortable when using them, but over time your skill level will develop. Also, once you have become familiar with them you will then discover that the real skill is to know when and under what circumstances these tools and techniques should be employed.

THE NATURE OF PROJECTS

This section aims to help you understand what a project is. It will provide you with a definition and then examine the key characteristics together with the uncertain and complex nature of a project. The section concludes with an overview of the project life cycle and the role of the project manager.

What is a Project?

Project management is not a new discipline. If we look to the ancient civilizations' constructions it can be seen that the human race has been undertaking large-scale and complex projects for thousands of years. It is difficult to imagine that these enterprises, like building the pyramids of Egypt, could have been achieved without some degree of planning and control.

To plan and control a project, managers need to create a model that describes its complexity along a time line to make sure that it will achieve its goals. This model of the project or plan can then be used to check the project's progress as it proceeds, to control the project. The first project to be managed in a way we would recognize as project management was the Manhattan project, which created the first atomic bomb.

If we consider these enterprises we can define a project as:

> *A series of activities designed to achieve a specific outcome within a set timescale and uses a defined set of resources.*

In this definition the most obvious project characteristic is achieving a specific outcome such as building the Channel Tunnel or landing a person on the Moon (and returning them safely to Earth). These are, of course, grand and memorable projects but launching a new product or reorganizing the Accounts Department still have a defined outcome that we know has or has not been achieved. It is also useful to think of a project as an instrument of change – it impacts people's lives by changing the nature of their work or their environment, which makes it harder to do than managing the status quo.

In addition to the specific outcome (scope, objective, goal) the other two key distinguishing features are that a project is time bound with a defined start and end to it and that its resources (time, money, people, equipment and so on) are defined. This is altogether different from *business-as-usual* which will be a routine set of processes that are followed on a day-to-day basis, for example, administering the payroll – a very important activity but not a project. Even organizations that are project-based, as in consultancy, will still have routine processes, such as accounting and finance, which support the business.

Mini task

Take a moment to think about all the different tasks you undertake at work (and home if you wish). Which are managing routine work and which are projects? Are there any tasks in the routine list that would be better managed as projects?

If you think there are some tasks that would be better tackled as a project do a quick sanity check against the characteristics listed in Figure 4.1.

In addition to the below characteristics, projects usually require a team of people to get the job done and their needs and desires also need to be addressed and managed.

Characteristic	Points to Note
Specific Outcome There is a measurable outcome; something is delivered.	This may not be clear at the outset and time often has to be spent to gain clarity and verify the desired outcome. Be aware of other (hidden) agendas. To increase the likelihood of success, objectives (goals) must be identified for all those involved in the project.
Set Timescale All projects have defined start and end points.	Routine work can be distinguished from projects because it is recurring and there is no clear start or end point to the process. A project is often initiated as a result of a report or resolution from a committee. Some projects are repeated. However, they are not *routine work* because they have clear start and end points, may use different resources and the desired outcome may change between projects.
Defined Set of Resources Projects are allocated time, people and money on their own merits.	All projects require separate resources, whether or not they have been set up as outside routine business. These may not be clear at the outset and time must be spent to ensure clarity, as working within agreed resources is vital for a project's success.
Instrument of Change Projects bring about change to work practices and/or the environment.	Projects impact the lives of people. It is often the people aspects of the project that have a significant influence on its success or otherwise. People have to be managed through the change.

Figure 4.1   Main Characteristics of a Project

An Example of a Project (*The Usual Suspects*)

The cinema has provided a wealth of material to study both successful and unsuccessful projects. This example of a project is taken from MGM's Oscar® winning film, *The Usual Suspects* (1995) – I am sure you can think of many other examples. If you have seen the film all to the good, but it is not vital to your understanding.

In the first part of *The Usual Suspects* the team of *villains* played by Stephen Baldwin, Gabriel Byrne, Benicio Del Toro, Kevin Pollak and Kevin Spacey, wished to steal some emeralds being illegally imported into the USA from a courier who was being transported by New York's Finest Taxi Service (Corrupt New York Policemen) to the exchange point.

The initial proposed plans all appeared to be *fatally* flawed as there was a high probability that there would be loss of life, which was counter to the desired outcome. After a number of discussions amongst the team, they adopt Verbal Kint's (Spacey) project plan as the one most likely to succeed. And, the project's successful execution earned Verbal the title of "The Man with the Plan".

Figure 4.2 illustrates some of the elements of his plan against the various project characteristics already shown (Figure 4.1).

Characteristic	Example from *The Usual Suspects*

Specific Outcome There is a measurable outcome; something is delivered.	This may not be clear at the outset and time often has to be spent to gain clarity and verify the desired outcome.
	
	   – *Acquire the emeralds without **any** loss of life.*
	
	Be aware of other agendas.
	
	   – *Keaton (Byrne) also wished to have the corrupt police exposed to repay them for ruining his legitimate business.*
	
	To increase the likelihood of success, objectives (goals) must be identified for all those involved in the project
	
	   – *Everybody on the team was to receive a share from the sale of the emeralds.*

Set Timescale All projects have defined start and end points.	Routine work can be distinguished from projects because it is recurring and there is no clear start or end point to the process.
	
	   – *The project formally started once there was agreement amongst the Team to undertake the venture.*
	
	A project is often initiated as a result of a report or resolution from a committee.
	
	   – *The project planning was initiated as a result of a report by McManus (Baldwin), given after the Usual Suspects had been interrogated at the Police Station. Some projects are repeated. However, they are not **routine work** because they have clear start and end points and the desired outcome may often change between projects.*

Figure 4.2   **Examples from Verbal Kint's Project Plan**

	– *There were similar projects, robbing a drug dealer and attacking the boat in San Pedro Harbor. Each of these had distinct start and end points and different desired outcomes.*
Defined set of Resources Projects are allocated time, people and money on their own merits.	All projects require separate resources, whether or not they have been set up as outside routine business. – *This type of villainy is a project-based business, stealing the emeralds required a specific set of resources - vans, guns and petrol in addition to the five men.* These may not be clear at the outset and time must be spent to ensure clarity, as working within agreed resources is vital for a project's success. – *A detailed plan was produced which included almost split second timing to ensure a successful outcome.*
Instrument of Change Projects bring about change to work practices and/or the environment.	Projects impact the lives of people. – *The corrupt police were exposed, lost their jobs and went to prison.* It is often the people aspects of the project that have a significant influence on its success or otherwise. – *Because of the surprise element, the police running the taxi service chose not to, or were unable, to fight. Had they done so the robbery (project) would not have achieved its objective.* People have to be managed through the change. – *Keaton had not wished to get involved in the robbery and Verbal was required to convince him that the past (going straight) was over and there were greater opportunities for him in the future if he took part.*

Figure 4.2   *Concluded*

A Project Topology

The definition of a project can be extended a step further. Projects are usually *complex* in terms of size and the number of people and resources involved and *uncertain* in achieving the project objectives of cost quality and time. Figure 4.3[1] illustrates a typology for projects according to their complexity and their uncertainty.

The topology helps to illustrate the vast array of undertakings to which project management can be applied. Uncertainty, in terms of the cost, schedule and technologies, will particularly affect project planning whilst complexity will have a significant affect on project control. For example, if I am to write a book on project management there is only one person involved and I can be reasonably certain about the associated times and costs. Compare this to obtaining a GATT agreement where many nations are involved some of whom may fail to ratify the agreement or attempt to renegotiate at every opportunity. Politics is a very uncertain business.

---

1   Adapted from Slack, N. *et al.* (1998), *Operations Management*, Pitman Publishing.

Uncertainty						
High		Basic research				GATT agreements
			Antarctic expedition		Military campaign	UN campaign
		Oil exploration				
		Product development		Airport		Channel Tunnel
		Stealing emeralds	Company audit	Chemical plant	Motorway	Airbus
	Writing a textbook	A Wedding		Oil tanker		Car plant
Low	Individual	Group	Organization	Multi-Organization	Nation	Multi-Nation
	Low		Complexity			High

Figure 4.3   Project Topology

Projects with high levels of uncertainty are likely to be extremely difficult to define and to set objectives. Often the project objectives will be evolving, and planning needs to be flexible with contingency plans incorporated into the implementation to allow for the consequences of change. By adopting a structured framework for project planning, the risks, assumptions and critical factors can be incorporated to ensure that contingency plans, when required, can be drawn up in advance of implementation

Projects with high levels of complexity need not necessarily be difficult to plan (the process of *chunking* a project will be described later) but it may require a lot of effort. Controlling them can be very problematic as you may be dealing with a large number of groups of people undertaking lots of activities that may have interdependencies on each other. When things start to go wrong the problems can grow at a phenomenal rate as the knock-on effects of one activity on another come into play.

Mini task

Draw a project topology chart. Consider what projects you and your organization are working on at the moment. Place those projects on the chart. Consider the implications for their planning and on-going control. List any actions you should take to address the issues that may have surfaced – you may wish to finish reading the book before you take any action!

Why Use Project Management?

Today's business world is highly competitive and it is imperative that managers deliver results on time and within budget. The preceding sections should have also provided you with an appreciation of both the characteristics and nature of projects and why they need to be managed effectively.

Adopting a project management approach enables you to identify and then focus on the priorities, track performance and overcome difficulties. Project management tools and techniques will assist you to exercise more control, so that you achieve your objectives on time and within budget. Time spent planning and organizing activities into project may appear to be a major effort at the outset, but you will be saving time and effort in the longer term and also reducing the risk of failure.

Stages of a Project (The Project Life Cycle)

It is worth outlining a form of structure for a project, for whatever the project you may undertake it will pass through a number of distinct phases. The nature of these phases will differ depending on the type of project, its complexity and uncertainty. This is also true for the time taken to go through each phase, which can vary from a few minutes to several years. As I have already indicated a project may begin as a result of a report or a feasibility study – which may have been projects themselves. Usually these will have defined the problem or desired outcome, for example, *"Steal the emeralds from the courier,"* and it may have a recommended course of action, *"whilst he is being ferried by the NYPD."* As the project manager it is your job to convert the proposal into reality, and in doing so you will take your project through five main stages:

1. Understanding the Project Environment.

2. Project Definition.

3. Project Planning.

4. Project Build and Implementation.

5. Project Review.

Stages 1 and 2, Understanding the Project Environment and *Project Definition,* constitute the pre-planning phase and they are probably the most important stages of your project because you are laying the foundations on which your project plan will be constructed. Quality time and effort spent pre-planning will ensure you are able to construct a realistic and robust project plan that will ensure a successful execution.

During these stages you will gain an understanding of your project's history together with how the organization's culture, structure and processes will influence it. You will clearly define the vision/mission/goal that the project is supporting and from that determine the project's terms of reference, set objectives, agree budgets and gain support for the project. This phase concludes with you determining the detailed requirements (*what* is required) and producing an agreed Requirements Specification or Terms of Reference signed off by the customer. During Stage 2 you will be working closely with your customer to gain complete clarity of precisely what they want you to deliver.

At the end of Stage 2 you should also review the project with the sponsor and ensure you have approval to proceed further.

Stage 3, Project Planning, is where you translate the *what* into the *how*. Subject matter and technical experts will assist your conversion of the Requirements Specification into a Detailed Design, which will in turn determine the overall project structure and the activities that are necessary to achieve the customer's required outcome. You are then able to produce a detailed project plan, which should include the risks/assumptions you have made together with anything identified as critical to the project's success.

At the end of this stage you should review the plan with the project's key personnel, particularly the sponsor and customer, and obtain agreement to continue.

Stage 4, Project Build and Implementation, is where something tangible is being created that on its completion will be handed over to the customer. Your focus will be on monitoring and controlling the project and preparing the organization for any changes that come about as a result of its implementation. Once you and the customer are satisfied with what has been delivered you can close this stage. But the project has not ended; you need to capture what has been learnt.

Stage 5, Project Review, is the stage where you and your team take time to review how the project has progressed, what has been learnt during its life. You should capture the learning in a way so that you and others can be more effective the next time. It is worth noting that these activities also map on to many of the 75 Ways mentioned earlier.

Your Role as the Project Manager

Your role in this venture will be similar to the role of any manager, you will:

- Plan;
- Organize;
- Co-ordinate;
- Control;
- Lead.

But what distinguishes you from a process manager is that you are fulfilling these roles in order to bring about a change, not manage business as usual. You will be focussed on achieving the project's aim.

You are also the primary interface between the project and the rest of the organization and you need to employ excellent communication skills to work with your sponsor and team, manage the customer's expectations and promote the project at every opportunity.

Because every project is unique you must adopt a systematic approach, or you will not have consistency in their management. Fortunately there are tools and techniques available to help ensure you adopt such an approach.

THE FIVE STAGES OF PROJECT MANAGEMENT

This section will systematically take you through the main stages of a project. It will examine the key activities you should undertake and provide some tools and techniques that will assist you in your project management role.

Stage 1. Understanding the Project Environment

This stage, because of our natural desire to demonstrate activity and immediate progress, is often either forgotten about completely or relegated to a minor part of the planning activity. We do so at our peril!

There are two key elements to this stage. The first is around understanding the background to the project and gaining an appreciation of how the organization will behave towards it and the second part is identifying the key players who will be involved with the project.

Environmental background

Before you start rushing around doing things sit back and start by considering the project's complexity and uncertainty and ask yourself:

- Has the organization done anything like this before?

- How clear is the project outcome?

- What is the organization's track record of achievement?

- Who might be the allies and the enemies of the project?

- Have there been any other similar projects? What happened to them?

- Are there competing projects?

- What is the current business climate like?

- Does the organization have the necessary skills and technologies?

- Where is the leadership?

- How do we resource projects?

- What is the customer like?

- Who will be on the team?

- How compelling is the project?

- What would happen to the organization if the project does not proceed?

If you do not know the answers find someone in the organization who can give you some pointers. The very act of thinking about these types of issues at the outset will start your mind running, so that when you commence the detailed planning phase you are more likely to have considered all the potential risks, assumptions and critical success factors that may impact the project.

A Killer Environment

A large telecommunications company wished to embark upon a major change programme. On reviewing the project environment it became apparent that the senior managers, who would be required to show leadership, were not united behind the project, even though their public words were to the contrary. In fact, the underlying culture was of distinct fiefdoms each of which was bent on ensuring the other divisions did not gain any advantage. It was a killer culture for any major interdivisional projects and until this fundamental issue was addressed there would be no progress.

Key players

As previously mentioned you, as the change leader, will also have to think about who are the key players and their roles in the implementation project.

Projects may involve a wide range of people with differing skills and backgrounds. As the project manager you are responsible for the entire project but you cannot succeed alone and the establishment of good relationships with other key players is vital for the project's success. In the previous section we examined some of your roles. We will now consider a number of other key roles that are common to all projects. How these roles are positioned in an organization will depend on its culture and structure. The way previous projects have been organized will provide you with a good guide for your project. A typical set of project key players, project stakeholders, and their roles is shown in Figure 4.4

The various project roles were undertaken for jewel robbery and these are illustrated in Figure 4.5. In the film the five first came together in the police cells and whilst they were incarcerated McManus took the opportunity to inform the others of the forthcoming opportunity.

Key Player	Roles
Sponsor Initiates the project and is accountable for its outcome. They will be the most senior person on the team.	Provides inspirational leadership. Ensures the project is relevant to the organization's needs. Assists in setting the objectives and defining constraints. May be a resource. Can be useful at managing "political" issues.
Customer The person who is the major beneficiary of the change brought about by the project.	Key influencer of the project's objectives. Key determiner of whether the project has been a success. May dictate how some of the activities are undertaken. May provide direction to the project manager. May provide resources for the project.
Affected Groups Any other party affected by the outcome of the project.	May influence the project's objectives. May be involved in determining whether the project has been a success. May provide resources for the project.
Project Manager The person who is responsible for achieving the project's objectives and leads the project team.	Produces the project plan. Leads and develops the project team. Monitors progress and instigates appropriate action to manage issues/problems and changes. Communicates project information to all interested and affected parties (i.e. To all the key players and their staff).
Project Team Member Any person who has actions to carry out in the project plan.	Is responsible for completing activities specified in the project plan. The project's size and complexity and the member's experience will determine the extent of their responsibility, for example, team leader.
Supplier/Contractor The provider of goods and services needed to carry out the project.	Delivers goods and services on time and at the cost agreed with the project manager. Can become very involved with and supportive of the project.

Figure 4.4   Project Key Roles and Activities

Following their release the group met up again to discuss the project's feasibility during which Verbal took the role of project manager and recognizing he needed five people to ensure the enterprise's success, he then worked hard to convince Keaton that he must join them in the venture.

Mini task

Consider a project you are about to commence or currently undertaking. Draw a picture/cartoon of what the environment is or will be like for the project, highlighting potential areas of concern to you. Draw up a list of the people who are/will be involved in the project categorising them according to player types. Look at your areas of concern and consider how the key players you have listed can help you address your concerns. If there are any concerns still left, consider whether any other players need to be introduced to help deal with them.

Key Player	Roles
Sponsor Initiates the project and is accountable for its outcome. They will be the most senior person on the team.	**McManus** He initiated the project having done a brief feasibility study with Fenster (Del Toro). The two of them will also arrange to sell the emeralds after the successful robbery.
Customer The person who is the major beneficiary of the change brought about by the project.	**All Five Usual Suspects** They benefited with a share of the emeralds.
Affected Groups Any other party affected by the outcome of the project.	**The NYPD Drivers and Courier** The corrupt policemen lost their jobs. The courier lost the emeralds and his money.
Project Manager The person who is responsible for achieving the project's objectives and leads the project team.	**Verbal Kint** "The man with the plan" He worked out exactly what resources were required for the plan to succeed. He ensured they were available.
Project Team Member Any person who has actions to carry out in the project plan.	**All Five Usual Suspects** It needed five men to carry out the robbery and each had a key role in ensuring its success.
Supplier/Contractor The provider of goods and services needed to carry out the project.	The supplier(s) are not known but guns, vans and a can of petrol were needed for the robbery.

Figure 4.5   Example from *The Usual Suspects*

Stage 2. Defining the Project

Having a clear idea of what the project will achieve is essential if you are to accomplish something of perceived value. Often a project is part of a programme, a series of projects, and it is critical to ensure that there is congruence not conflict across them. To ensure this you will work during this stage to:

- Define/understand and agree the project goal/vision and how it relates to any other organizational goal(s), particularly if your project is part of a programme of projects.

- Define the project specific objectives.

- Define scope and boundaries of the project.

The hierarchy of objectives

In defining and agreeing your project vision/goal you will need to involve the project sponsor, customer and members of your team. It should aim to be a succinct statement describing the result or outcome of the project. Always be as audacious as possible within the confines of the overall organizational goals. A simple example of a hierarchy of organizational goals is illustrated in Figure 4.6. The overall organizational goal is to improve profits by 20 per cent and this goal was translated into two key programmes, one focussing on Cost Reduction and the other on increasing Market Share. The Cost Reduction programme in turn cascaded into a series of sub-programmes that themselves were made up of a series of specific project objectives, like Achieving Zero Defects.

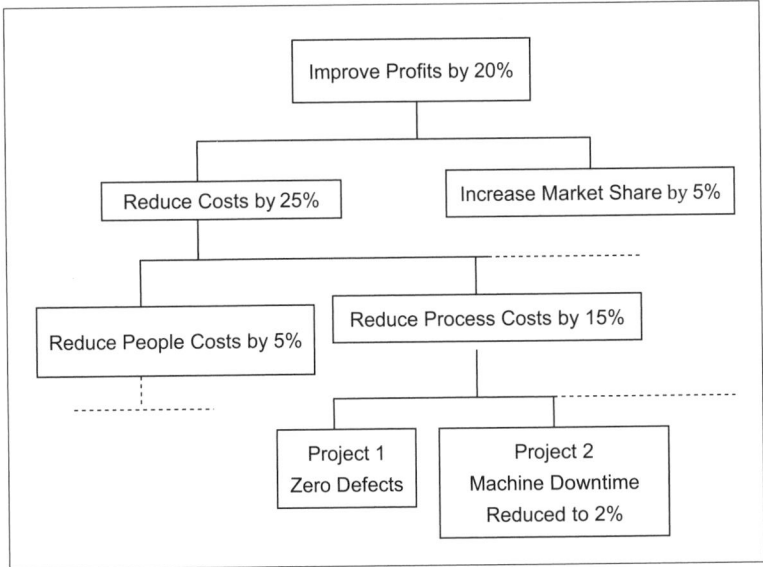

Figure 4.6   Goal/Objective Hierarchy

At this point, you may be wondering if there is any difference between programme and project management. Programme management provides an umbrella under which several projects can be co-ordinated. It does not replace project management, but is a supplementary framework that must be underpinned by effective project management and project reporting mechanisms. Programmes have the vision of the end state, but no clearly defined path to get there; projects are on route to achieving the vision.

Mini task

Examine the goal/objective hierarchy in Figure 4.6 and make a list of what you believe to be wrong with the way they have been stated. Revisit your list at the end of the section. Make a list of all the different reasons you can think of for setting project objectives.

Project objectives

You have seen that the alignment of objectives should be explicit and that the project objectives should describe precisely how it contributes to the business. Additionally your project objectives should also be SMART:

Specific;

Measurable;

Agreed Upon;

Realistic;

Time-bound.

Specific – Your project objectives should be clear, not vague or general. If they are vague you will not *really* know whether or not they have been achieved.

Measurable – These measures of success are the touchstone of the project objectives. A project to improve productivity should state how much extra will be produced and/or what the cost savings will be. They should be measurable in terms of quality, quantity, time, cost and the defined end product.

Agreed Upon – The best way to ensure that the project objectives are agreed upon is to ensure they are consistent, readily understandable and are few in number.

Realistic – It is in your interest that the objectives are realistic and achievable. You must satisfy yourself that this is the case. There is nothing wrong with audacious objectives, but there can be significant morale and motivational side effects if the objectives are perceived by your project team as unrealistic.

Time Bound – It should be clear in what time frame the project objectives are to be achieved. For example, Zero Defects to be achieved by 30 June 2012.

If you are presented with vague objectives one method of clarifying them is to break the project down into three categories – purpose, end result and success criteria. For example, the earlier objective of "Machine Downtime Reduce to two per cent" could be broken down into:

Purpose – To ensure that production meets its forecast output targets.

End Result – A report which identifies the causes of machine downtime and which recommends how this can be reduced to 2 per cent or less.

Success Criteria – The report should be completed by 26 October. The recommendation should enable output to reach 10,000 units per month. The cost of the recommendations should not exceed 75K Euros.

Finally, with SMART project objectives aligned to the organizational goals you are much more likely to obtain the full support and commitment of all the key players as they should:

- communicate the project's purpose;

- provide direction;

- provide a focus on the results;

- enable plans to be made and work prioritised;

- motivate staff;

- and, most importantly,

- enable success to be recognized.

Project scope and boundaries

The second part of a project's definition is the project's scope. The scope of a project is essentially a boundary or constraint setting exercise that attempts to set out the dividing lines between what each part of a project will do. It aims to clarify the responsibilities of all the parties involved in the project. Defining the scope of a project or sub-project will usually be helped by defining the parts of the organization that are affected, the time period involved, the business processes involved, the resources to be used and the extent of the solution provider's responsibilities. For example, in a project involving developing a web site pilot the scope was given as follows:

Parts of Organization Affected – Environmental Division.

Time Period – To begin no earlier than 1 October and completed no later than 22 December.

Business Processes Involved – Press release process, report publication and distribution process.

Resources to be used – Two members of Information Services and one member of the Environmental Division.

Responsibilities – To include all end-user training.

Objective consistency

Projects can be defined by three performance objectives – cost, time and quality. It is worth spending some time testing that these objectives are consistent for your project. All too frequently business objectives, on which your project may be based, contain short-term contradictions such as increasing shareholder returns whilst increasing investment in new plant and equipment. In circumstances where there appear to be contradictions you should state what the project priorities are and where any trade-offs may take place. Not forgetting to test them with your sponsor and customer.

When determining the trade-offs consider which is the overriding performance objective and explore how the other two can be adjusted to achieve the prime objective. This is called analysing the objectives triangle. Figure 4.7 illustrates a selection of different prime project objectives. Projects where the well-being of humans are involved, like astronauts, would have a high emphasis on quality, whereas cost would be the focus for delivering a fixed price contract and time for an advertised rock concert. It would be a poor situation if people arrived for the Glastonbury Festival to find cows roaming the fields but no bands, sound stages or toilet facilities. This would not be the experience they paid for.

As a project manager you will be constantly engaged in some form of trade-off during a project. Where you position yourself will depend on the overarching objective at that time, this will be examined more fully during the Execution stage.

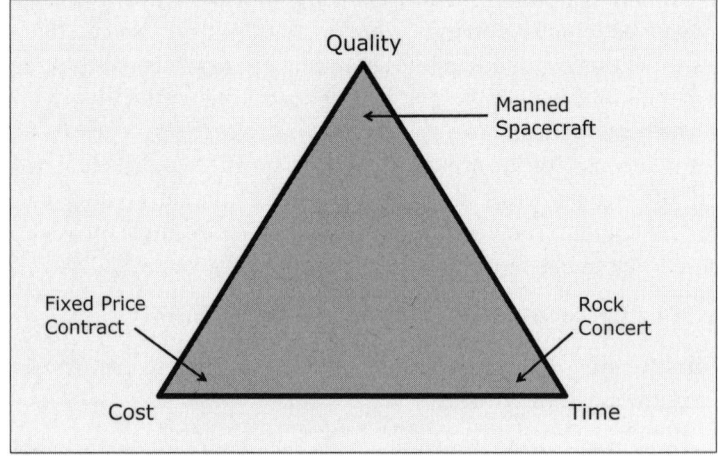

Figure 4.7   Project Objectives Triangle

Mini task
Review your current projects and decide which is the prime objective for each one. Consider the likely tensions between the prime objective and the other two. What action, if any, should you be taking now to ensure the tensions remain manageable?

Project specification
The scope of a project is formalized in its project specification. This document defines the project output, the accompanying terms and conditions, and will be signed-off by the customer to indicate agreement. During the life of a project you will discover that the scope may well change from what was originally specified. This could be because you or your team may have identified better/different ways to execute the project, or your customer has changed their mind. The former is called an internal change and the latter an external change. In a commercial project it is important to distinguish between these two types of change as you can demand payment for external changes, but not internal ones.

Project strategy

Having spent time considering the project's environment, objectives and scope you will see how the project is beginning to take shape. You can now define, in broad terms, how you consider the project should be undertaken and complete the final part of the project's definition, the project strategy.

The project strategy will define the key phases you envisage the project will pass through together with any significant milestones. These milestones will be used during the project's execution to determine whether the project is on schedule, to cost, and to quality. At this point you will not determine the detailed timings and costs associated with each milestone, as this is carried out during the project's planning stage.

The project framework

The project framework, Figure 4.8, is based on the Logframe Approach, developed by Leon J. Rosenberg, under contract to USAID. It is used extensively by NGOs and is an excellent way to summarize and present your pre-planning work. By completing every box in the Framework you will have the basis (foundation) for a well planned and executed project. As you can see it provides a tabular illustration of most of the elements that have been discussed during this section. It depicts the objective hierarchy by showing the organization goal to which the project contributes to, along with other projects. The goal has been decomposed down as far as the key activities that will be undertaken during the project. Figure 4.8 also shows the factors critical for its success, identified perceived risks, any key assumptions that have been made and, most importantly, it captures which are the key performance indicators and their evaluation method(s).

Results Hierarchy	Performance Indicators	Monitor and Evaluation	Assumptions/ Risks	Factors Critical for Success
Goal: Higher objective to which the project, along with others will contribute	Measures to verify accomplishment of the Goal	The programme evaluation system. Data sources to verify the programme status	**Goal to Super Goal** Assumptions regarding strategic impact	**Goal to Super Goal** Critical factors regarding strategic impact
Purpose: The effect or impact of the project	**Impact:** Measures that describe the accomplishment of the Purpose	Sources of data needed to verify the status of purpose level indicators	**Purpose to Goal** Assumptions needed to attain Goal	**Purpose to Goal** Critical factors that will affect attaining the Goal
Outputs: The deliverables of the project or terms of reference	**Achievement** Measures to verify the accomplishment of Outputs	Sources of data needed to verify the status of output level indicators	**Output to Purpose** Assumptions needed to attain Purpose	**Output to Purpose** Critical factors that will affect attaining the Purpose
Activities: The main activity cluster that must be undertaken in order to accomplish the Outputs.	**Input/Resources:** Budget by activity, monetary, physical and human resources required to produce outputs	People, events, processes, sources of data and monitoring system for validating the activities' status	**Activity to Output** Assumptions that must prevail in order to achieve Outputs	**Activity to Output** Critical factors that will affect attaining the Outputs

Figure 4.8   The Project Framework

In Figure 4.9 the framework has been applied to *The Usual Suspects* example given the super goal of "To live a long life", with the project support goal of "To retire from crime". The project scope has also been extended to include the sale of the emeralds.

Results Hierarchy Super goal – To live a long life	Performance Indicators	Monitor and Evaluation	Assumptions/ Risks	Factors Critical for Success
Goal: **Retire from crime**	• Regular job • No crime for 5 years	• Wage slips • Tax returns • Police wanted list	**Goal to Super Goal** • No contact with old friends	**Goal to Super Goal** • Remaining healthy
Purpose: **Increase bank balance**	**Impact:** • Money available for pension fund	• Measure bank balance • Measure value of fund	**Purpose to Goal** • Past rates of return continue in the future	**Purpose to Goal** • They are not with a bogus pension company
Outputs: **Cash**	**Achievement:** • At least 50 emeralds at safe house • Sale Value > $100K	• Count and verify the number of emeralds in presence of all team members • Count cash	**Output to Purpose** • Money is shared amongst team	**Output to Purpose** • Each team member has a bank account
Activities: **Acquire intelligence** **Plan** **Obtain resources** **Steal emeralds** **Lie low** **Sell emeralds**	**Input/Resources:** • $500 for informant • $2000 for equipment • 5 men	**Check there are:** • A detailed plan • 4 vans • 5 guns • Can of petrol • 5 men	**Activity to Output** • Good intelligence from informant • Able to sandwich police car • High quality jewels	**Activity to Output** • 5 men • Police don't shoot • An "honest" fence for the emeralds • Not recognized by anybody

Figure 4.9 *The Usual Suspects* **Project Framework**

A critical review of each box will indicate where the team should focus their planning effort and if some sub-projects need to be set up to ensure the risks are managed. Milestones may be set against the Activities which will decompose further during the Planning stage. You will note that the project Output is not just a restatement of the Purpose and that there may be a need for interim measures such as checking bank balances as well as the longer term one of measuring the value of the pension fund.

Terms of Reference

By the end of the pre-planning phase you should have a good idea of what the project is all about and be in a position to contract with your customer and sponsor. Creating a set of Terms of Reference for the project will define the project's context and should include:

- Project sponsor;
- Customer;
- Authority under which the project will be conducted;
- Project objectives;
- Project scope;
- Constraints/boundaries.

- Budget or anticipated costs;

- Resources;

- Project outcome/deliverables;

- Project strategy including phases and key milestones;

- Risks;

- Roles and responsibilities.

Go/no go

The preparation and agreement of the Terms of Reference by your customer and sponsor is an important project milestone. The work you have done so far will provide key information concerning the project's viability and enable the decision to proceed or otherwise to be made. If there is agreement to proceed then you will move to the detailed planning stage. Alternatively there may be modifications to the scope, objectives and/or budget and by doing so revise the Terms of Reference before proceeding or there may be a decision not to go ahead with the project.

A Cautionary Tale Concerning a Political Project

A division of a major electronics company decided that it required a new materials management system. Having completed the pre-planning a set of Terms of Reference were submitted to the project review board. The analysis had indicated that a 10 per cent reduction in stock costs would be achieved as a result of the new system being introduced. Unfortunately the cost estimates for designing, developing and implementing the new system far exceeded the benefits that would accrue from the 10 per cent stock reduction. The project would therefore fail the company's financial investment tests.

But, the review board wanted this project to proceed, so they decided that there would now be a 12 per cent reduction in stock costs and this new figure just happened to satisfy the investment tests.

The project proceeded and, because the project board continually changed the project specification, it cost significantly more than the original estimates. To overcome this financial problem the benefits expected to accrue from the new system were, yet again, revised upwards and a degree of "creative accounting" introduced to satisfy the post project audit.

Today the company no longer exists.

Stage 3. Project Planning

Having completed the pre-planning phase you are now able to undertake the detailed planning for your project. Please remember that planning is not a one-off exercise that is finished when the plan is issued. There may, because of changes of circumstances, be occasions when you re-plan the project several times. This often happens if you are dealing with a complex project of some considerable duration. As time goes on you obtain more information, activities become less uncertain and the assumptions you made at the outset may no longer hold true. In these circumstances you will find yourself re-planning.

Earlier in this chapter we identified the following five stages of a project:

1. Understanding the Project Environment.

2. Project Definition.

3. Project Planning.

4. Project Build and Implementation.

5. Project Review.

Although creating the project plan and then executing it is an iterative process, you may like to consider these stages as a simple process (Figure 4.10), with a Project Control function providing sensing/control mechanism, via the dotted lines, with feedback loops to the earlier stages.

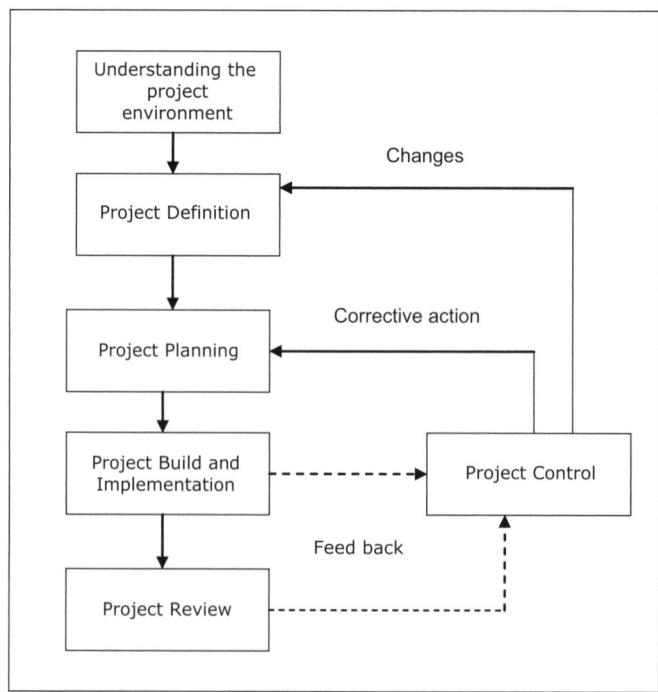

Figure 4.10   A Project Management Model

Feedback concerning the project's performance may result in the need to re-plan the later activities. Significant variances between the planned and actual performance may require the project to be redefined and the Project Review stage may result in changes to the way we plan and control future projects. Re-planning a project is not a sign of failure; it demonstrates that positive action is being taken when the circumstances necessitate it.

Your project planning will fulfil four distinct needs:

1. It determines the cost and duration of the project.

2. It determines the level of resources that will be needed.

3. It allocates work and identifies who is responsible to enable progress to be monitored.

4. It helps assess the impact of any changes that may occur.

Work Breakdown Structure (WBS)

The pre-planning activity of producing a project's Work Breakdown Structure is key, as it forms the basis of much of the remaining planning activities such as setting budgets and assigning responsibilities.

Most projects require breaking down – *chunking* into a manageable, mind-sized, series of activities (Figure 4.11). Each package of work (Activity) within the structure may then be assigned its own objectives in terms of time, cost and quality. It is also crucial to identify for each activity the people who will be **R**esponsible for doing the work and **A**ccountable for its outcome. If a third party's input is required or someone needs to be consulted, then this **S**upport should also be recorded. It may be necessary that we keep someone, for example, a steering group or senior executive, **I**nformed during the work's execution or, depending on the politics, there may be someone who has to be **M**anaged to ensure things go smoothly. This is called applying the RASIM (Figure 4.12), to each activity. Once completed, we will have a very clear picture of the people aspects of the project.

The aim of the Work Breakdown Structure is to bring real clarity to the project and provide an information management schema for reporting purposes. As project manager it is unlikely that you have all the necessary knowledge and subject matter expertise to undertake this task alone. You will need to involve other people in helping you salami slice the project. The number of levels you arrive at in the breakdown structure will depend on the project complexity. Try to keep things mind-size. Up to six levels are probably OK, if there are seven or more then you should consider creating sub-projects and if they reach double figures the project's scope is probably too great. The nature of the outcomes and outputs from activities will differ as one moves down the project hierarchy. At the higher levels there are likely to be distinct project phases with major deliverables. At lower levels the activities will be of shorter duration and are less likely to stand-alone. At this level you must be very clear

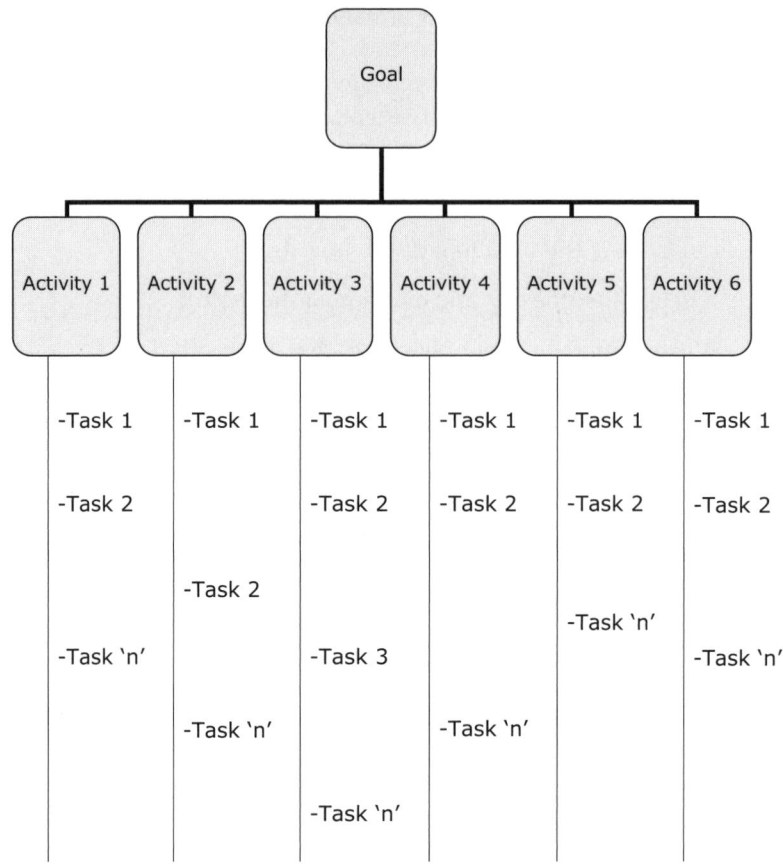

Figure 4.11   A Work Breakdown Structure

Who is **R**esponsible for doing the work
Who is **A**ccountable for its outcome
Whose **S**upport is needed
Who needs to be kept **I**nformed of progress
Who needs to be **M**anaged

Figure 4.12   Applying RASIM

about what is to be delivered and the activities should have the following characteristics:

- It must be measurable in terms of cost, effort, resource and time.

- Result in a single verifiable deliverable.

- Have clear start and end dates.

- One person should be accountable.

Figure 4.13 illustrates the single level Work Breakdown Structure constructed from *The Usual Suspects* Pre-Planning Project Framework. The boxes are the main project phases identified using the Framework.

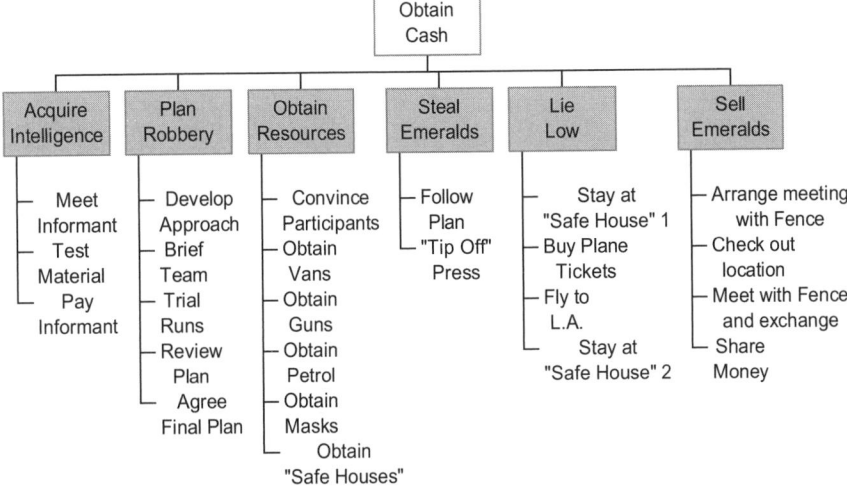

Figure 4.13   Single Level WBS for *The Usual Suspects*

It is a good practice to codify the activities so they have a unique identifier, which in turn can represent the structure. For example:

A. Acquire Intelligence.

A1. Meet Informant.

A2. Test Material.

A3. Pay Informant.

B. Plan Robbery.

B1. Develop Approach.

B2. Brief Team.

B3. Trial Runs.

And so on, until all of the project is codified.

Completeness

Having reached this point it is also helpful to enlist the aid of a colleague to act as a sounding board to your project logic. Go through the planned activities step-by-step to check that nothing is missing or that you have assumed something is listed. Then, as a final check, test whether all the activities listed are really necessary.

Organizing and documenting resources

Once you have established the Work Breakdown Structure you have a reasonably detailed view of the project and what needs to be done. The next step is to determine who is going to do what and how they should be organized. You will be making estimates and asking others to estimate the time, effort and cost associated with the various activities as well as identifying other resources, for example, rooms and equipment that are necessary to support the activity.

Estimating

With experience you will get to know those people who are optimistic when doing estimates and those who are pessimistic. Both of these types of estimate are dangerous, the over optimistic one means you will probably run out of time and too many pessimistic ones may result in the project failing to clear the financial hurdles and senior management deciding not to proceed. You will need to discuss the basis of the estimates and negotiate with those who are accountable for the delivery of activities. If estimates appear too long, is the estimator trying to make life easy for themselves, or are they over-engineering the solution (producing a Rolls-Royce when a family hatchback would do)? If estimates appear too short, does the estimator really understand the complexity, the quality level of the deliverable or have unreasonable assumptions been made? Always ensure that necessary skills/competences are included in the activity description to ensure that during execution the right type of resource is applied to your project, not just anybody.

Estimating principles

If you follow the principles outlined below you are more likely to have acceptable accuracy:

- Estimates should be honest.

- Estimates should be in terms of days effort (person days). The elapse time to complete the task is (days effort/number of appropriate people undertaking the task) plus an allowance for any known constraints, for example, difficult working conditions.

- The skill and experience level of the people undertaking the activity should be allowed for.

- Estimates should not include any contingency allowance that can be applied at a global level.

- Any assumptions should be documented.

- During the life of the project check the assumptions made still hold true.

- You must always seek the commitment of all individuals involved in the activity and also do the final sanity check of asking yourself, "Does this appear a reasonable estimate?" If not, re-open your dialogue with the estimator.

With experience you may develop some general rules of thumb for your projects. For example, you may have discovered that if the Design Phase of a certain type of project takes three months, that the Build Phase then takes six months, that is a ratio of 1 to 2. If the estimate for a similar project indicated a Design Phase of two months and a Build Phase of two months, then it is probably worth undertaking a short investigation to understand why the Build Phase is much faster.

Dependencies

On most projects some activities may be performed concurrently (in parallel) and some must be done in a distinct order (in series), for example, you need to have acquired the vans *before* you undertake the robbery.

Defining the dependencies is defining the order in which activities should be done. You do this by starting at the end of the project and then work your way backwards to its beginning. At each activity you ask yourself, "What must be in place before I can start this activity?" You will then establish predecessors for every activity until you arrive at the beginning. This is not a trivial exercise, as you will discover activities dependent on multiple predecessors or other complications such as some activities that may require starting at a predetermined time after others. The basic types of dependency are:

Finish to Start – the preceding activity must be completed before the succeeding one can start.

Start to Finish – the preceding activity must start before the succeeding one can finish.

Finish to Finish – both activities must finish simultaneously.

Start to Start – both activities must start simultaneously.

Having determined your project's structure, obtained estimates for each activity and identified the dependencies you may then prepare a Project Resourcing Matrix and Dependency Network, Figures 4.14 and 4.15, which all the project stakeholders can review and ultimately agree upon.

Schedule constraints

Once you have estimates of the time and effort required for each activity and identified their dependencies, it is then possible to compare your project's requirements with the resources available. The resources available for your project will not be infinite and some, such as specialist skills or test equipment, may be in short supply and need to be taken into account during the planning process. You may be required to undertake some detailed re-planning to account for these constraints. It is possible for activities in your project to be resource constrained, the available resources cannot be exceeded, or time constrained, it must be finished at a given time and once the resources are used up, alternative ones are scheduled. The earlier Rock Concert example from the Project Objectives Triangle (Figure 4.7), serves to illustrate the time constraint point. Once the bands are booked and the date of the concert is advertised the project is time constrained. If during the project execution phase any activities, such as building the sound stages, are not going to finish until after the go-live date then additional resources will need to be deployed to meet the scheduled completion date at the same level of quality.

To help you manage resource-constrained projects it is worth constructing a matrix (Figure 4.14), that indicates where and when the scarce resources are being deployed. In this example, for Week 27, there are three people with common critical skills working on activities for Projects A to D. New Project E would need to be re-planned from its original Week 27 schedule as there are insufficient resources available.

Week 27	Project A	Project B	Project C	Project D	Project E	Utilization
Requirement (Person weeks)	0.75	0.50	1.0	0.75	0.50	
Smith	0.5	0.5				1.0
Dubois	0.25		0.25	0.5		1.0
Chan			0.75	0.25		1.0
Total	0.75	0.5	1.0	0.75		

Figure 4.14   Resource Planning Matrix

You are now in a position to create your resourcing matrix (Figure 4.15) for all the key activities. Figure 4.16 shows one Verbal might have prepared for *Obtaining Vans* activity.

WBS Activity Code	Activity Name						

Deliverable (description)						Quality Level	

Who is Accountable			Start Date		End Date		

Dependencies			
Activity	WBS Code	Dependency Type	Who is Accountable

Resourcing		
Days Effort	Skill/Competencies	Who is Responsible for doing the work

Other Requirements	
Training	
Facilities	
Equipment	
Materials	

Costs		Other Roles	
Staff		Project Manager	
External Suppliers		Customer	
Professional Fees		Who is Consulted	
Other		Who is kept Informed	

Total			

Additional Information

Prepared by		Department	
Telephone		E-Mail	
Version		Date	

Figure 4.15   Project Resourcing Matrix

WBS Activity Code	Activity Name					
3.2	Obtain Vans					

Deliverable (description)					Quality Level	
Four Ford Transit or equivalent size vans					Mechanically Sound	

Who is Accountable	FENSTER		Start Date	2/4/94	End Date	4/4/94

Dependencies				
Activity		WBS Code	Dependency Type	Who is Accountable
Team Briefing		2.2	Finish to Start	VERBAL

Resourcing			
Days Effort		Skill/Competencies	Who is Responsible for doing the work
2		Car Theft	Car Stealers Inc.

Other Requirements	
Training	None required
Facilities	Garage close to Safe House 1
Equipment	Slim Jim, screw driver – To be provided by Car Stealers Inc
Materials	HT Wire – To be provided by Car Stealers Inc.

Costs		Other Roles	
Staff	–	Project Manager	VERBAL
External Suppliers	$5000	Customer	The TEAM
Professional Fees	–	Who is Consulted	McMANUS
Other	–	Who is kept Informed	VERBAL
Total	$5000		

Additional Information
False licence plates to be provided. Vans should not be in colours or with sign writing that would draw people's attention to them.

Prepared by	VERBAL KINT	Department	Confidence Tricksters
Telephone	999-9999-9999	E-Mail	verbal.kint@conmen.com
Version	1.0	Date	25 March 1994

Figure 4.16   Project Resourcing Framework for *The Usual Suspects*

Creating a dependency network

A dependency network is a pictorial representation of the relationships between the project activities and visually shows which ones depend on the completion of others. These are also known as PERT (Program Evaluation and Review Technique) charts or network diagrams. The PERT methodology was developed by the United States Department of Defense for its Polaris submarine programme. This visual presentation can enhance your understanding of the project and enable you to:

- Determine the shortest time in which the project can be delivered.

- Determine the critical path.

- See activities that may represent a risk (for example, an activity that introduces a bottleneck).

- See periods in the project when too many activities may be happening (too much complexity).

The minimum information shown on such a chart would be the activities, their dependencies together with their start and end dates. Apart from simple projects most project managers tend to use an automated project planning software package to produce their network. The software does the number crunching leaving you with more time to spend analysing the results. Figure 4.17 shows a dependency network for *The Usual Suspects*.

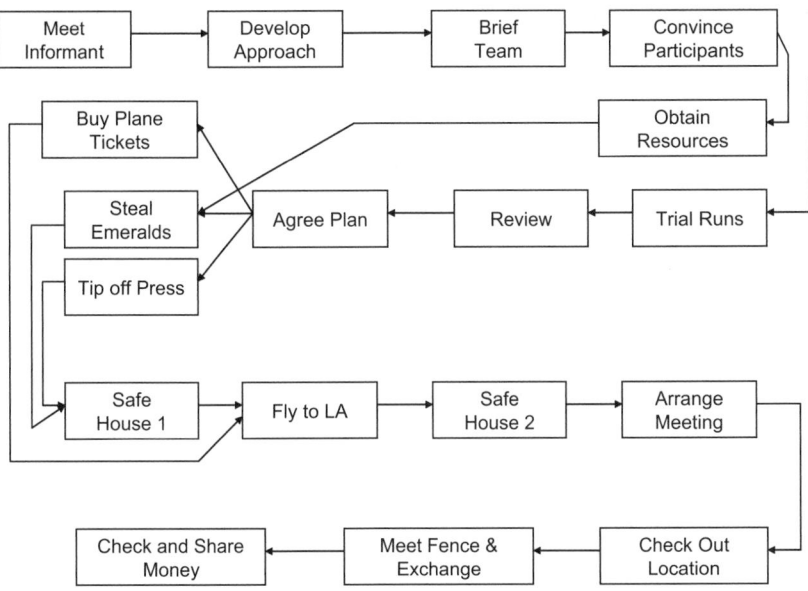

Figure 4.17   Dependency Network for *The Usual Suspects*

The network provides a top-level map of how the project will run and illustrates that you cannot steal the emeralds until you have an agreed plan and all the necessary resources. Buying the plane tickets to Los Angeles could be undertaken as soon as the plan was agreed or just before going to the departure lounge at the airport. Knowledge of the availability of tickets may influence when it should be done.

There are a number of conventions for drawing your network. The illustration (Figure 4.18) is for the Activity on the Node method (that is a box, the node, represents the activity and the activity information is contained within it).

Earliest Start Time	Activity Duration	Earliest Finish Time
Activity Code Number		
Activity Description		
Latest Start Times	Total Float	Latest Finish Time

Figure 4.18 **Activity on the Node Convention**

When using a software package you will enter each activity's description, code and duration together with the dependencies. The system will then calculate, for a given project start time, the earliest start and latest start and finish times for each activity and its float, or slack time, which is the amount of time it can be delayed without affecting any other activities or the end date of the project.

Figure 4.19 illustrates the completed node for *Obtain Vans* in *The Usual Suspects* project. If the project started on 1 April then the earliest start time for activity 3.2 *Obtain Vans* would be 6 April and the latest finish would be 11 April. The float for the activity is four days being the difference between the earliest start and latest start dates.

6 April	2	7 April
3.2 Obtain Vans		
10 April	4	11 April

Figure 4.19 **Activity on the Node for *The Usual Suspects***

Slack (float) in your plan may be beneficial because it may allow you some latitude for planning when activities should be done to enable the smoothing out of resourcing peaks.

Critical path

The critical path is established by tracing a line along the dependency network through those activities that have no slack. This trace represents the path through the project where if any slippage occurred then the project completion date would also be delayed. This is also the shortest possible time in which the project can be completed. It is the critical path activities and other ones near the critical path that you, as the project manager, should concentrate your efforts on to ensure that they go well. And, in the real world of project management there are bound to be resource constraints, like Week 27 for Project E (Figure 4.14) when you may have to make decisions about which is the most important project and whether or not resources can be transferred from another project, or staff work overtime, which will increase the project's cost. You will soon discover that good negotiation skills are a key competency of the effective project manager.

The Gantt chart

The Gantt chart (Figure 4.20) is the main tool that you will use for scheduling your project and then controlling it. The chart lists activity information on the left-hand side and the project time scale across the top. The activity bar is a line that graphically represents the time period during which the activity will be executed. It is an excellent idea to also include the activity's WBS code and who is accountable for its delivery. The Gantt chart is a good communication tool, particularly illustrating the higher levels of the project structure with each bar showing the start and finish dates for each part of the project. The chart may also be used to illustrate the project's actual progress with those members of *The Usual Suspects* team who are accountable for achieving the phase outcome.

Contingency

Some activities will include a contingency for specified risks. However, it may not be possible to identify and include every eventuality that can harm the project. After you and the team have considered all the major risks to the project and taken steps to minimize their effect you may wish to introduce an across the board contingency for the project. This should be clearly stated and included in the project costing.

Validating the plan

The final activity in the Planning Stage is to review the Plan, Networks, Charts, Resourcing Matrices and other supporting documentation with the project's major stakeholders.

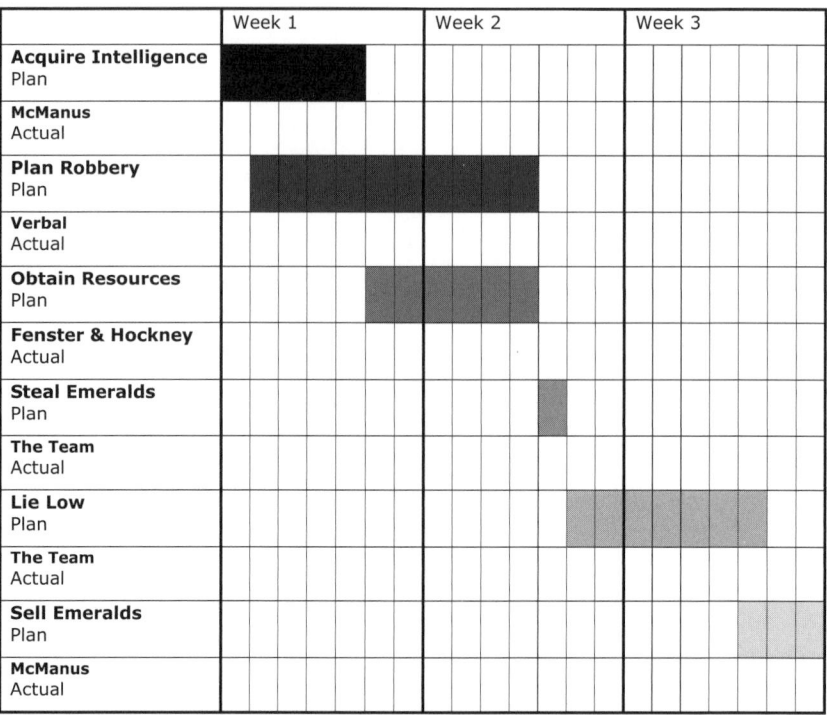

	Week 1	Week 2	Week 3
Acquire Intelligence Plan			
McManus Actual			
Plan Robbery Plan			
Verbal Actual			
Obtain Resources Plan			
Fenster & Hockney Actual			
Steal Emeralds Plan			
The Team Actual			
Lie Low Plan			
The Team Actual			
Sell Emeralds Plan			
McManus Actual			

Figure 4.20   *The Usual Suspects* **Gantt Chart**

At this review everybody should be clear about the project timings, costs (budget) and responsibilities and the final go/no go decision for the project will be made.

Your plan can now be executed.

Stage 4. Project build and implementation

Planning and organizing your project may have seemed to be quite intense, but it is the controlling of your project that will consume most of your time. During this stage there are two key activities that you will undertake:

- Monitoring the project to check on its progress.

- Control by assessing the project performance against your plan and intervening in the project in order to make changes that will bring it back on to your plan.

Project launch

However, before you commence these activities you will need to launch the project formally. During the earlier phases you will have involved the various stakeholders in the development of the plan. Successful execution requires you to keep everyone involved effectively engaged. To achieve this you will need to continue building, developing and leading your team to convert involvement to commitment.

Involvement or commitment

There follows a short story that helps to illustrate the difference between being involved in a project and being committed to it.

Involvement or Commitment

A hen and a pig were thinking about how they might go into business together. One day they were passing a factory just as the night shift was leaving. They both noticed that the workers looked tired and hungry as they traipsed past them; and this gave them an idea. Why not set up a business to provide egg and bacon breakfasts to the hungry workers? You can immediately see from this, that whilst the hen was involved in the venture, the pig was committed!

Almost everyone has the need to feel included in something that is larger than them; we like to be part of a group or team and preferably a successful one. Use the launch to get as many of your team together, remind them of the project's objectives and how it fits into the wider organization's goals and super goals and get them to meet one another. Aim not only to get them committed to the project but to secure commitment to each other.

Note: If you have someone imposed on your project who is a *team killer*, make them an Executive Consultant or whatever title you think is appropriate so they can be an individual contributor and you manage their interaction with the rest of your project team.

Project monitoring

First you have to decide what you should be looking for as the project progresses. The project objectives triangle of quality, cost and time is a good starting point and the project framework will also provide you with the specific outcomes.

Time

At various points during the planning stage of your project you will have publicized the key milestones and their dates, which makes you very keen to ensure they are met. Consequently you will wish to know in advance of reaching each milestone how the project is progressing and so you will need to monitor the activities that contribute to the milestone and scrutinize their progress.

The key time-related data you will be interested in will be:

- Project status (awaiting to start, started, completed).

- Elapsed time spent.

- Person days effort spent.

- Estimated effort required for completion.

- Estimated elapse time to completion.

You can then compare this information with your original plan – something that most project management software tools will automate for you. From your perspective the two critical pieces of information are the estimates for the Required Effort and the Elapse Time to complete. By comparing these with your plan you can easily identify if an activity has slipped.

Cost

As with time, costs can be used to measure progress; very important when the project budget is tightly capped. During the planning stage you will have developed resourcing profiles for the activities and you will also know the external costs, like consultancy and equipment purchases. One cost you need to pay particular attention to is the cross-charge from other departments – particularly if staff incentives depend on the level individuals are employed on projects.

A Tale of Cross-charging

The Systems Group of a major corporation's IT function was responsible for current systems support and new systems development for each of the corporation's companies. After several growth years the corporation entered a difficult trading period and one of its responses was to introduce a cost reduction programme that included cutting the systems development budget by 25 per cent.

The Systems Group, rather than reduce staff numbers or find alternative external development work, responded by booking more of their time to systems support codes – whether the systems really needed supporting or not. Because the charges were spread over a large number of cost centre codes within the Group each code only showed a slight overspend. Consequently it was some months before the impact of the "mis-charging" was discovered, which resulted in the cost reduction programme failing to achieve all of its goals. The following year the corporate IT function was disbanded, but that may have been purely coincidental!

For controlling your project the three most important cost figures are:

1. Estimated costs at Completion (EAC) – The total cost of the project or activity based on the costs incurred to date plus future scheduled costs.

2. Budgeted cost at Completion (BAC) – The total budgeted costs for the project or activity.

3. Actual cost of work performed – The amount of money spent so far.

The comparisons should be based on the amount or value of the work done and future work requiring to be done. Do not use the project's time lines to calculate these costs.

Quality

Measurement may not be as easy as time or cost and the views of quality will vary with the type of project. The key thing is to ensure that the quality standard is defined at the outset and a plan is in place to ensure the standard will be met. This plan should include:

- The standard for each deliverable.

- The procedures and processes to be employed to achieve the required standards.

- The project checkpoints.

- The standards for supervision and review.

Reporting progress

Typically you will select some key areas to keep a close eye on to provide you with an early warning of future problems. Once you have managed a few projects you will have become aware of the three fundamental laws of project management:

- When a project appears to be going well, something will go wrong.

- When things cannot get any worse, they will.

- When things appear to be going better, you have overlooked something.

You will collect data about your project's performance from a number of sources including:

- Regular written progress reports – typically weekly or monthly.

- Formal progress meeting (one-to-one or group).

- Direct primary data.

- Wandering about – informal.

Written progress reports

Create a standard template for your regular reports, for example, the 3Ps format:

Progress – Accomplishments since last report.

Problems – Identification of deviations from plan and the actions being taken to compensate.

Plans – Specifying the major activities and goals for the next reporting period.

Or SOFT format:

Successes – Accomplishments since last report.

Opportunities – Major goals to be achieved for the next reporting period.

Failures – Deviations from plan and actions being taken to compensate.

Threats – Issues/Problems that look likely to occur in future reporting periods with proposed actions for their resolution.

For both formats the entries under each heading should be succinct with the detail contained in the report's appendices, for example, financial data, key milestone data and commentaries.

Formal progress meetings

It is good for the members of the team to meet with each other and you formally. Your leadership skills will be key to ensure that these meetings do not degenerate into beat-up, "isn't it awful?" or "aren't we all wonderful?" sessions as none of these approaches will help you control the project. You could consider following the same format as the written reports, with the attendees briefly describing their progress, problems and plans. Use the meeting to focus the individual or group on the key tasks at hand, undertake some joint problem solving and explore opportunities. Always conclude the meeting on a positive note.

Direct primary data

This type of data is your early warning of things to come, for example, the purchasing function advising that world prices for a key component have changed, or a team leader advising that a key member has become incapacitated. In these circumstances, having checked the data's validity, you can start planning your course of action prior to being told at any regular/ periodic progress meeting.

Wandering about

Wandering about helps you develop a *gut feel* for your project. You will have an idea of what you expect to be happening at a particular time and if it is not then you will wish to find out why not. Wandering about is the distributed version of the open office door. Project team members will feel they can approach you during your walk about and just stopping to talk about the weather can help lubricate the team dynamics.

Project control

Having gathered information the project manager has to decide what is to be done to see that the project reaches a successful conclusion.

The 80/20 Rule

A civil engineer friend of mine, who I consider to be an expert project manager, reckons he spends 80 per cent of his time wandering around keeping his eyes and ears wide open and 20 per cent of his time reading project reports, attending project review meetings and using his project support software tools. Over the years he has developed an instinct for seeing problems long before they manifest themselves in the formal reports. In this way he deals with many of them before they become "show stoppers".

If you have done a thorough job planning the project you will have confidence in your ability to deliver it to time, cost and quality. However, things will always happen a little differently to what you had originally expected. There are many factors that can change your project, for example:

*   The requirements may change.

*   The completion date may change.

*   The budget may change.

*   Your planning assumptions may have been wrong.

*   Mistakes are made.

*   Key resources might not be available.

*   Incorrect/inaccurate estimates.

*   Organizational priorities change.

*   Fire, flood and so on.

Most problems can be resolved if they are caught soon enough, which is why regular and honest reporting is paramount. When problems do occur you will need to take action by:

*   Assessing the situation and its risks/impact.

*   Resolving the issues and problems.

*   Managing the change.

Assessing the situation

When a problem occurs you need to assess its impact and determine what action, if any, needs to be taken. One assessment method is to build a Fishbone diagram (so named because it looks like a fish skeleton). You put the problem/issue as the head and then build up a skeleton as you assess its impact. Figure 4.21 uses *The Usual Suspects* example to offer a diagram of the event of them missing the flight to Los Angeles. The consequences might be that they would be unable to meet the fence to sell the emeralds and that by staying in New York there is an increased likelihood they would be found by the police. The chart then continues to expand to record the two key impacts of missing the flight – they do not receive any money and they go to jail. Armed with this information they can make a dollar-value impact assessment caused by missing the flight, which can assist them in deciding how much they might spend to minimize the impact.

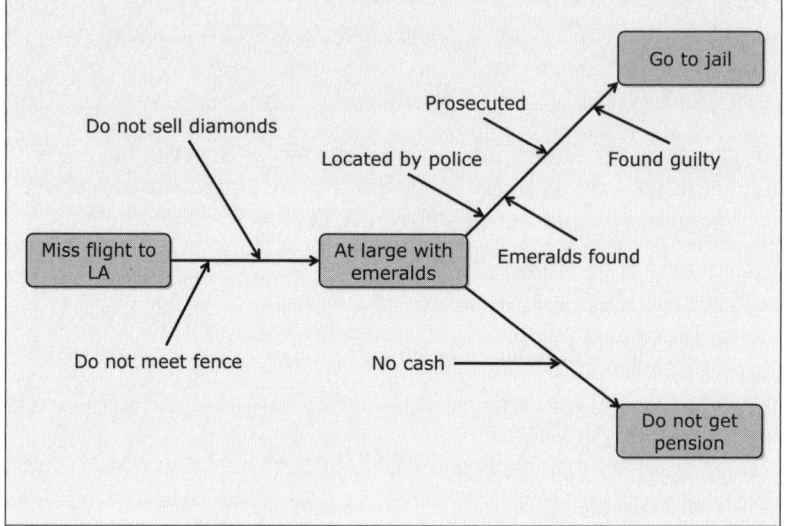

Figure 4.21   **Impact Analysis Adapted Fishbone Diagram for *The Usual Suspects* Crime**

The diagram can also be expanded to the left of the issue box to brainstorm all the possible causes of missing the flight. You can then decide what action should be taken to eliminate the potential causes. This type of analysis may also be undertaken when you are completing the risk/assumption and critical factors columns of your project framework. Having completed the analysis you may decide that you should undertake additional activities or sub-projects to minimize the risks to your project.

Whenever possible get a member of the team, with appropriate knowledge, to help you undertake the assessment.

Automated project tools that come with project management software packages can assist you to try out a number of different scenarios and calculate different end dates and costs.

Resolving the problem
When faced with a major problem, for example, missing the flight to LA, there are a number of potential routes that you may explore to help resolve it.

First of all you should consider what happens if you do nothing. This does not mean ignore the problem, because they do not go away of their own accord, but provides you with baseline data against which your solutions may be compared. For, it would be unfortunate if you spent more on resolving the problem than leaving it alone.

Creative solution

Next you should try to see if you can identify a creative solution. You may have a sudden flash of inspiration as you lie in your bath, but the solution is more likely to appear from you revisiting your plan and planning assumptions. Has anything changed that might allow you to undertake some of your planned serial activities in parallel? Are the constraints that existed at the start of the project still applicable? Can you introduce some new or better technologies?

Contingency

During planning you had the foresight to build in some contingency for this eventuality. However, it cannot be used a second time and once it has all gone, it's gone. So use it only when you really have to and monitor and control it very carefully.

Cost, quality and time

One or more of the planning objectives triangle's three elements of cost, quality and time may be relaxed. You may apply more resources to address the problem – this will increase cost. You may allow the completion date to slip – this will increase time or you may reduce the quality (or scope) of the deliverable. None of these are desirable actions but there will be occasions when there is no alternative. You will need to think very carefully about which one or combination of the three you will relax. Revisiting the prime objective may assist in determining how you should proceed. Spend time consulting with key team members, your sponsor and customer before making the final decision.

Learning

It is important, having resolved the problem that it does not happen again on this or any future project within the organization.

You should, therefore, examine the root causes of the problem and what measures can be put in place to prevent it in the future or, if it can't be prevented, its impact minimized. You will need to work on this with other members of your team and having identified a solution you must ensure that it is communicated to the rest of your organization.

Project change

There can be any number of reasons why there is a significant change to the original project plan. It may involve an amendment to the original terms of reference or even the project objectives. You will need to have a process for handling these key amendments and any requests for change. The process should include an impact and cost benefit analysis and a procedure, depending on the extent and impact of the change, for sign off by the customer and sponsor.

These changes must be managed, for if the project content is allowed to change too freely then the rate of change will always exceed the rate of progress. There must be a point in the project's life when it has to be frozen, no matter how unpopular with the user, and no more changes accepted.

Costly Change

A major supermarket chain, when reviewing its new store building costs, was surprised to discover that their regional directors, by modifying the new store's layout "to meet the changing local market conditions", during the last four weeks prior to opening were imposing a significant cost on the project. A cost that outweighed the sales benefits derived from the changes.

Stage 5. Project review

As your project draws to a close it is important to evaluate what has been achieved and what has been learnt. Once the project has completed you should check:

- If the project sponsor is satisfied that the project's objectives have been met.

- If the customer is satisfied with what was delivered.

- What has been learnt from the project?

Normally you will hold formal meetings with the sponsor, customer and project team members. Take the opportunity to thank everybody who has been involved in the project. Whenever possible have an event to celebrate the project's success, to show both recognition of the team's effort and to provide an opportunity for disengagement and farewells.

Your final task is to prepare a closedown report. This should cover:

- What the project achieved against the original objectives.

- An explanation of any significant variances from the original financial and resourcing plans.

- An appraisal of what went well and what went badly during the project.

- Any key factors that will be of benefit to future projects.

- Ensuring that all insights and ideas are recorded.

Project documentation

You will add this report to all the other project documentation that you have been maintaining; be it one small file or many large filing cabinets full. A complete project document set will cover every aspect of the project and include:

- The Project Mandate.
- The Project Brief.
- Vision or Goal Statement.
- Your Project Blueprint – outline approach.
- The Business Case.
- Benefit Statements/Profiles and Delivery Plan.
- Communications Strategy and Plan.
- Financial Plan.
- Project Organization Structure.
- Quality Management Strategy.
- Risk Strategy and Log.
- Project Plan.
- Issues/Change Log.
- Project Policies and Procedures.
- Project Support Office Functions.
- Project Review.

And as one project file closes another one is opened.

PERSONAL QUALITIES OF THE CHANGE PROJECT MANAGER

Throughout this chapter we have been mainly looking at a change project in a mechanistic way and followed a change project management process from concept to delivery. Occasionally we have mentioned the main project resource, its people – the project team – and it is how the project manager works with the team that is critical to a project's success. When considering the personal qualities remember the FEE and LIPS model introduced earlier in the book and examine how necessary the qualities are to ensure change projects progress smoothly.

When I run seminars I often ask the delegates to draw a cartoon of the expert project manager. Each seminar some wonderfully creative pictures are produced followed by deep discussions into the nature of project management and the qualities that are needed to be successful. In addition to the technical aspects of project management four key personal qualities always emerge:

1. Leadership.

2. Communication.

3. Motivation.

4. Delegation.

Leadership is listed first because successful projects rely heavily on the loyalty and commitment of those who are involved. Team members are often seconded, sometimes on a part-time basis, and just being managed will not be sufficient to engage people correctly.

Effective communication is about having a flexible style and approach that meets the differing audience's needs. It is as much, if not more, about listening than talking, particularly as a project manager often needs to persuade and influence, not just be directive.

As project managers rarely have direct control over an individual's pay it is fortunate for them that financial remuneration is not a great motivator – though insufficient money or perceived remuneration inequalities can act as a demotivator. Expert project managers are skilled at achieving a good degree of alignment between people's personal objectives and those of the project and meeting the other broader human needs of:

• Belonging – to the project team.

• Feeling involved.

• Having interesting and challenging work.

• Having a sense of achievement.

• Being recognized for effort and successes.

• Having the opportunity to develop.

• Using their skills.

• Taking more responsibility.

To achieve this you must know your team members at a personal as well as business level.

Only with very small projects can the project manager undertake everything. The exemplar project manager recognizes that not only can delegation make their own life easier, but it can also make team members feel more involved and responsible for their work. It is all part of developing the team and when delegating the project manager will be very clear about what needs to be done, when it needs to be done by, why it should be done and how much authority they are giving.

These personal skills coupled with a good understanding of what running a project entails will improve your likelihood of success.

Appendix: Organizational Types

WHAT'S YOUR ORGANIZATION LIKE: JAGUAR OR MULE?

The research mentioned in the Preface, also helped to identify four organizational types, Figure A1, based on the levels of resistance and motivation that exists within an organization.

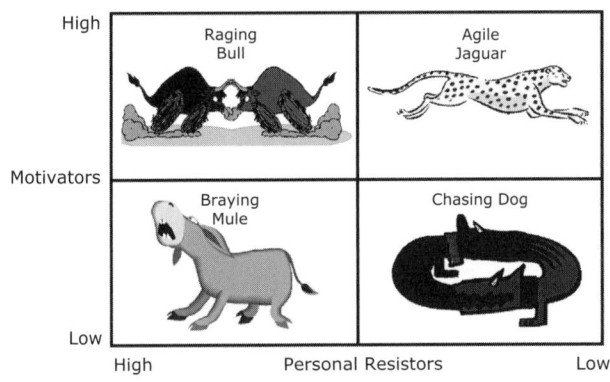

In which organization is there any "real" movement

Figure A1   **What Type of Organization Do You Have?**

These four types are:

1. **The Braying Mules organization** – where people are highly resistant to the change and management is providing very little motivation to change. In this instance there is a lot of noise being made by the people who do not wish to change and no movement, as they dig in their heels.

2. **The Raging Bulls organization** – where people are still highly resistant, but management are endeavouring to motivate them to change. In this instance there is a lot of energy (often heat and noise)

being expended by both parties that cancel each other out and again there is no movement.

3. **The Chasing Dogs organization** – in this instance people exhibit little or no resistance to change, that is they are up for the change, but management does not apply sufficient motivators. When the change is lacking in one or more of leadership, incentives, plans and/or sense of involvement, then there is no focus or direction. A consequence of this is that people are likely to do their own thing and the organization and its people just go round in circles.

4. **The Agile Jaguar organization** – people feel ready and able to change and motivators are appropriately applied that enable the organization to quickly respond to change. This type is the only Totally Change-Adept organization. None of the other organizational types is capable of making any significant forward movement towards achieving their goals.

The research also resulted in the creation of a Change Readiness Diagnostic tool that enables leadership teams to measure the degree of personal resistance to change, FEE, level of motivation, LIPS, and potential problem areas within their organization.

References and Suggested Further Reading

There are literally tens, possibly hundreds, of thousands of books that explore change. Below I have listed a short selection that I referred to whilst writing this book. They should provide a good starting point for your own exploration.

CHANGE LEADERSHIP

Belasco, J., *Teaching the Elephant to Dance*, Century, 1992.

Brooks Jr., F.P., *The Mythical Man-Month: Essays on Software Engineering*, Addison Wesley, 1978.

Covey, S., *Principle Centered Leadership*, Fireside, 1992.

Davis, S. and Meyer, C., *BLUR*, Capstone Publishing, 1998.

Drucker, P., *Management*, Heinemann, 1974.

Herzberg, F., Mausner, B. and Snyderman, B., *The Motivation to Work*, Wiley, 1959.

Kotter, J., "Winning at Change", *Leader to Leader*, 10, 27–33. Fall 1998.

Kübler-Ross, E., *On Death and Dying*, Touchstone, 1969.

Lock, D. and Harrison, F.L., *Advanced Project Management* (4th edn), Gower Publishing, 2004.

Maslow, A., "A Theory of Human Motivation", *Psychological Review*, 50, 1943.

Merrill, D. and Reid R., *Personal Styles & Effective Performance*, CRC Press, 1981.

Morgan, G., *Images of Organization*, Sage, 1989.

Moss Kanter, R., *The Change Masters*, George Allen & Unwin, 1984.

O'Day, R., "Intimidation Rituals: Reactions to Reform", *Journal of Applied Behavioral Science*, 10(3), 373–86, 1974.

Robbins, H. and Finley, M., *Why Teams Don't Work*, Texere, 2000.

Schwalbe, K., *Information Technology Project Management*, Course Technology: Thomson Learning Inc., 2002.

Senge, P., *The Fifth Discipline*, Doubleday, 1992.

Senger, P., Kleiner, A., Roberts, C., Ross R., Roth G. and Smith B., *The Dance of Change*, Nicholas Brealey, 1999.

Turner, J.R. (ed.), *Gower Handbook of Project Management* (4th edn), Gower Publishing, 2008.

Waterman, R., *The Renewal Factor*, Bantam Press, 1987.

Weisbord, M., *Organizational Diagnosis: Six Places to Look for Trouble With or Without a Theory*, Organizational Research and Development, Block Petrella, 1976.

About the Book

This book is based on research conducted over a decade, coupled with practical change project delivery experience from across a wide range of industries. It was initially written in support of the Achieving Business Change workshop and other change leadership events/programmes which have been delivered to a wide variety of organizations over the past 12 years.

It aims to be both pragmatic and practical in its approach and provides a range of tools, techniques and exercises. In this way the reader is able to employ these ideas to assist them deliver their own change programmes.

This book comprises four chapters following the Introduction: Chapter 1 examines some theoretical aspects of individual and organizational change; Chapter 2 develops the FEE and LIPS change model for successful change leadership; Chapter 3 provides 75 Ways a change leader can influence and sustain the transformation; and Chapter 4 assists the change leader in implementing and successfully managing the change project.

Throughout there are a number of suggestions and activities that the reader may undertake in support of a change project.

About the Author

Prior to founding The Learning Cup, Martin spent some twenty years in management consultancy and people development, working with a wide variety of organizations across Europe and the USA in both the public and private sectors. In addition to his consultancy/training activities he has given public lectures on Organizational Change and has also lectured on Business & IT and Strategy for Undergraduate, Post Graduate and International MBA programmes.

Martin is a member of the Association of Management Education and Development, the Institute of Directors and the Institute of Management Services. He is the author of a number of papers/reports including "Creativity and Innovation in UK Companies" and "The Cultural Revolution – Organizational Changes for the 90s", as well as writing a successful series of training and development books which are published throughout the world.

ChangeGame®

A training tool to assist the development of change leadership skills

ChangeGame® allows participants to first explore organizational change and leadership theory and then experience the "realpolitik" of introducing innovation and change into a complex organizational environment. It is an interactive simulation which runs on a laptop and enables individuals or small groups to embed their understanding of the principles of effective change contained within this book. Unlike real life, the simulation has a roll-back facility, hence it is possible to learn what doesn't work without any negative consequences for the organization.

WHAT IS CHANGEGAME® ALL ABOUT?

ChangeGame® was conceived following the successful implementation of a major organization change programme for a large UK company. It was developed to help organizations positively respond to change.

It is a rich experiential learning event that not only provides change leadership and management theory, exercises and a workbook, but also allows participants, using a realistic simulated organization, to experience some of the real and complex issues that are faced when leading an organizational change programme.

- It supports the development of leaders to drive and support change.

- It aids the empowerment of managers and their staff to achieve change.

- It underpins the strategic and tactical activities/projects undertaken to achieve change programmes.

- It helps you to learn and remember those key change leadership lessons, before costly mistakes are liable to be made or repeated.

KEY OUTCOMES AND EXPERIENCE

- Appreciate the simple complexity of the organizational change process.

- Manage the introduction of a major change programme.

- Team working.

- Project planning and resourcing.

- Manage organizational politics.

- Deal with unexpected critical situations.

- Understand that all actions require an investment of personal credibility.

- Understand that your credibility only increases when you deliver worthwhile results to the organization.

WHEN TO USE CHANGEGAME®?

Most projects fail because of the cultural, people and organizational issues – it is rarely because of the technology.

ChangeGame® helps people to appreciate and address these issues, so they can both lead and manage change successfully.

Use ChangeGame®:

- For developing change leadership at all levels of the organization.

- With project team members and/or their clients to remind them both of the typical issues they will face during the change.

- To support newly appointed managers and team leaders.

MATERIALS INCLUDED

- Achieving Business Change presentation and exercises.

- Self-paced computer based tutorials.

- The ChangeGame® computer simulation.

- Installation guide.

- System user guide.

- System tutorial.

- Facilitator guide.

- Complete delegate materials.

- Suggested event timings.

- Change theory and game briefing presentations.

- Critical situation exercises.

- Achieving Business Change handbook for delegates.

- Installation instructions.

HOW TO EXPERIENCE CHANGEGAME®?

ChangeGame® events may be delivered by:

- Licensed training organizations.

- Your own people development/training staff – once they have completed a "train the trainer" session.

WHERE HAS CHANGEGAME® BEEN USED?

During the past 7 years ChangeGame® has been used in support of management and leadership development programmes for a wide variety of organizations, both private and public sector including: Aliaxis, Bayer Pharmaceuticals, BT, Siemens, Bournemouth University, Civil Service College, Dumfries and Galloway Council, HM Customs and Excise.

> *The behaviours I observed during the exercise are similar to how our managers actually operate. And, for several teams, the simulation had become so "lifelike" that they wanted to keep on playing.*
>
> Helen Marshall, Head of People Development
> North Lanarkshire Community Services

For further information please contact: Adrian Banger (Master Licensee) The Paradigm Partnership Ltd, asb@paradigm-partnership.co.uk (www.paradigm-partnership.co.uk).

Index

If you have found this book useful you may be interested in other titles from Gower

59 Checklists for Project and Programme Managers
Rudy Kor and Gert Wijnen
Paperback: 978-0-566-08775-2
e-book: 978-0-7546-8191-5

Accelerating Business and IT Change: Transforming Project Delivery
Alan Fowler and Dennis Lock
Hardback: 978-0-566-08604-5
CD-ROM: 978-0-566-08742-4

Communicating Strategy
Phil Jones
Paperback: 978-0-566-08810-0
e-book: 978-0-7546-8288-2

Critical Chain
Eliyahu M Goldratt
Paperback: 978-0-566-08038-8

GOWER

The Essentials of Project Management
Dennis Lock
Paperback: 978-0-566-08805-6

Gower Handbook of Programme Management
Geoff Reiss, Malcolm Anthony, John Chapman,
Geof Leigh, Adrian Pyne and Paul Rayner
Hardback: 978-0-566-08603-8

Project Leadership
Second Edition
Wendy Briner, Colin Hastings and Michael Geddes
Paperback: 978-0-566-07785-2

Visit **www.gowerpublishing.com** and

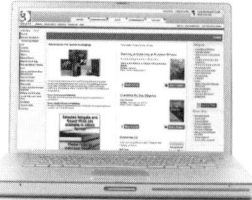

- search the entire catalogue of Gower books in print
- order titles online at 10% discount
- take advantage of special offers
- sign up for our monthly e-mail update service
- download free sample chapters from all recent titles
- download or order our catalogue